COUNSELLING IN THE COMMUNITY

Roger Altman is Director of Barnabas Training Consortium and Co-Director of Barnabas House, Wales. Both these organisations were founded by Roger and Glenys Altman, and between them they facilitate residential care, day counselling and counselling-related training. Roger has been involved in social work for over twenty years – lately as a senior manager. This work has included managing children assessment centres, residential homes, setting up new projects, supervision and training social workers. As part of this training he was involved with colleges and universities throughout the UK and was part of permanent planning groups and assessors.

Roger's primary work has included feasibility studies and the setting up of Christian and secular projects and training. The projects he has been involved with include counselling centres, residential centres for single mums, projects for the homeless, training centres, and promoting and establishing counselling in GP surgeries and Health Trusts.

In recent years his work has involved team building, management training and working with National Vocational Qualifications. At present Roger is a consultant trainer for Christian Action Research Education (CARE), Youth With A Mission, Elim Bible College, Assemblies of God Bible College, Premier Radio, Pioneer, and Crusade for World Revival. He is also working with various churches and Christian caring groups across the country. In addition to this he is Chairman of Training for the Association of Christian Counsellors and a member of the Executive Board.

*I would like to dedicate this book to my wife Glenys,
for her support and encouragement in working with hurting people;
and to Mrs Lyn Eastwood, my Personal Assistant,
for her research and dedication to good practice.*

Counselling in the Community

A Guide for the Local Church

ROGER ALTMAN

KINGSWAY PUBLICATIONS
EASTBOURNE

ISBN 0 85476 635 9

Designed and produced by Bookprint Creative Services
P.O. Box 827, BN21 3YJ, England for
KINGSWAY PUBLICATIONS LTD
Lottbridge Drove, Eastbourne, E. Sussex BN23 6NT.
Printed in Great Britain.

Contents

Foreword

Some years ago my wife Celia and I had a disturbing telephone call from a friend who was a social worker with responsibility for a number of disturbed teenage boys. It was late at night and he needed our help. One of the lads in his charge had so blotted his copybook that no Social Services establishment in the borough would have him. 'Please can you take him for the weekend and I'll find a home for him by Monday?' he asked. So with some fear and trepidation, we agreed. Actually David lived with us for the next three months! We discovered his basic approach to life was very different from ours and he caused us radically to think through many issues. It was an experience we shall never forget. I just wish we could have had Roger Altman's book then to guide us.

Roger has gained a real understanding of the social, emotional and spiritual problems which beset a growing underclass in our society and *Counselling in the Community* communicates both his thoughts and practical advice. With the divide widening between those who have been given so much and those in need, many individual Christians and local churches are concerned to offer care.

This book is not just an 'ought to be' but, more importantly, a 'how to' manual for us all. Counselling needs to be at the highest standard of professionalism so *Counselling in the Community* is a timely handbook for those with a heart to care. It deserves the widest possible attention because while not claiming to be *the* expert on the subject, Roger's qualifications, experience and Christian dedication are unique.

If we take heed of what Roger writes, the lives of thousands of people in need will be touched.

Lyndon Bowring
February 1996

Introduction

Looking at my personal experiences over the past twenty years I have seen tremendous joy and heartbreak with regard to the setting up of Christian counselling and caring projects within the pastoral and community settings. This manual will answer questions on the role and function of counselling in general and Christian counselling in particular. A clear vision and careful planning are essential for success, especially with regard to good practice. The guidelines contained in this manual will hopefully enable those involved in the setting up of various projects to clarify their goals, while also providing a useful tool to assist in the planning of these projects. The manual covers such areas as:

(a) Management structure
(b) Working with voluntary/statutory bodies
(c) Guidelines to the Children Act and Community Care Act
(d) Involvement with professional bodies
(e) Residential and day care facilities
(f) The pitfalls of planning permission and building regulations
(g) Professional involvement
(h) The role of the church in the community
(i) The importance of prayer and faith
(j) Planning ahead, both short and long term
(k) Counselling skills
(l) Legislation and ethics

For those beginning on the journey of setting up a project, this manual provides an awareness of the issues and pitfalls that those who have trodden the path before have encountered.

Within the church there has always been a tension between the preaching of the gospel, the primary task of the church, care for its members' physical and emotional well being, and the work of the church in the wider community. As I travel throughout the UK and other parts of Europe, I spend a considerable time looking at the work of the church in the community. On almost every street corner, or within each estate, there is a church building, ranging from a small hall to a cathedral. In many cases these buildings are closed and locked, and on enquiring of those living in close proximity about the work of these churches the response is often that very little is seen. Even trying to contact ministers and church leaders is often difficult because of their reluctance to talk about the church in the community. There has been a massive increase in what is known as the 'house church' movement. These churches can be even more difficult to find as they tend to use cinemas, village halls, leisure centres and other venues. In discussion with the ministers/leaders I have often found that they expect the people to come to them, and if these people actually attended their church they would then attempt to meet their personal needs. We are now faced with the reality that as we head towards the year 2000 and beyond, we are dealing with an unchurched generation. In order to reverse this situation churches will need to become more pro active within the community. One of the ways forward is for the church to open its doors to the community so that the gospel can be shown in a loving and caring manner to a generation that has lost direction and is caught up in a materialistic world.

Up to this point I have painted a rather gloomy picture of the church, but I am aware that many churches are opening their doors, refurbishing and/or extending their buildings and then offering their building to the community for a variety of uses. This may just mean renting the premises out for nurseries, playgroups, luncheon clubs, meetings for the elderly or housebound, or to Social Services. All of this is a very good beginning, but in many cases it does not meet the needs of the whole person. I realise that there are churches and organisations which are working to meet these needs in the community by offering counselling, working with single parents and mothers and toddlers, helping with drug- and AIDS-related problems, supporting the abused and providing a whole range of day and residential care. From our history we have seen tremendous strides made by those churches that are prepared to open their buildings to a wider use while taking care not to lose the ethos of a place of sanctuary or worship. We can see this from National Children's Homes, Barnardo's, National Society for the Prevention of Cruelty to Children, Shaftsbury Society and many others. I often wonder if these organisations were about to start up today whether today's church or community would step out to meet the need, or whether society in general, with all of its legislation and discrimination, would allow the church to function in a manner that would bring glory to God. As well as all this there is the government ideology of seeking voluntary private organisations to take over roles normally associated with the state (although some churches see this as an opportunity rather than a cause to lament government policy).

Indeed, over the last decade we have seen some growth in the number of people who are prepared to work in the church setting and wider society. These include organisations such as AIDS Care Education and Training (ACET),

Teen Challenge, Promoting Christian Child Care and
Action (PCCA), Christian Action Research Education
(CARE), Living Springs, Barnabas House, Crisis Centre
Bristol, Hebron House, Christmas Cracker, and others. We
have also seen a growth in Christian counselling agencies
throughout the country and the inauguration of the Association of Christian Counsellors. I am sure there are many
I have not named that have made significant steps working
in the community.

A growth has also been evident in training organisations
operating within the church and the community. Some of
these are commonly known as para-churches and many
offer exceptionally high standards of good practice. These
include Christian Services Training Centre, Waverley
Abbey, Caring for Life, Christian Action Research Education, Network Counselling Bristol, Manna House North-
ampton, The Lighthouse Coventry, Crossline, Philippi
Trust, Barnabas Training Consortium, Youth With A
Mission, and some of the theological colleges.

Within our society individual Christians, churches and
trusts have built centres offering a multitude of services to
the church and the community. These have included
nursing homes, day and residential care, counselling,
therapy, prayer ministry and healing. For the majority,
where there has been a vision, prayer, waiting on God
and a well-thought-out business plan, there has been
success. In other cases where there has been a vision or
heart's desire or response to a need, without the laying
down of foundations in prayer, waiting on God, counting
the cost or drawing up a business plan, there has been
failure and many have not lasted more than three years. If
we are to approach a secular society and talk about what
we wish to achieve in our 'salt and light' ministries, it is
important that we realise we must adopt a responsible
manner.

One of the major factors that Christian organisations should be aware of is that there is only a limited amount of finance within the Christian community, and this fluctuates according to world needs. In an attempt to alleviate suffering in worldwide crisis points some Christian organisations will move finance around from one need to another with very little notice, thus causing potential for financial difficulties in many local projects. I realise that much of the work of Christian organisations within the UK may be seen as 'faith' work, but money is still being provided by individuals, groups and churches that can be affected by changes in the economy. However, where there has been faith many projects have come into being with no initial finance whatsoever. My own bank manager has often been amazed by the way Christian projects have opened and survived in the appalling recession of the 80s and 90s. However, I am also aware of the many that have not survived and in some cases where Christians have over-stretched themselves in their vision or have not planned correctly. The loss of homes and livelihoods has been the result. The overall economic climate and the loss of employment in many areas of the professions and industry has had a knock-on effect with regard to financial support for Christian projects.

Considerations should be given to the working out of a short- and long-term business plan in all Christian projects. This should include faith, prayer, a financial business plan, a team plan and outside consultants. Many evangelical organisations also have fund-raisers. They may be called consultants, or personal representatives, but in reality if we are to be totally honest they are fund-raisers and as such they are expected to bring in finance, with some having pre-set targets to reach. Some Christian organisations are in fact using secular methods to raise funds, such as collection boxes in shops, fund-raising days and sweet boxes. In my opinion there is nothing wrong with these methods so long as the organisations concerned do not then state, 'We work by faith.' As I help new organisations to come into being, I often hear language which is quite triumphant, or aims and objectives which are far beyond their capabilities. For example, one organisation said that it was going to set up an alternative to the NHS; another said that it was going to become the Christian equivalent to Relate, and yet another said that it was going to consider setting up a Social Services Department. In an ideal world it would be good to have Christian services in all areas, but we must realise that many of these things would cost millions of pounds, take a lifetime to build and many, many years of training.

One of the biggest problems Christians have in setting out plans for the future is that they do not take into consideration that those who appear to be stepping out on the journey with them may not necessarily have the same vision. Within a short time a split or division arises causing many a new church or Christian project to close. As one purchaser of services said to me, 'The one problem I have with Christian organisations in the UK is that they are here today and gone tomorrow,' and sadly this is often due not to the lack of finances but to splits and divisions within these churches and organisations. He went on to say that he was not prepared to invest time, finance and more importantly people's lives into such organisations until they grew up or became more mature. This is a very sad indictment, but unfortunately in many cases it is true. If we are to build into the community from a Christian perspective we need to have short- or long-term goals according to the type of project we are setting up. We must realise that if we are going to build into hurting people's lives they will need to be able to rely on a consistent service – just as the local GP surgery is always open within its stated hours.

Those setting up projects also need to be aware that it can be relatively easy to raise money for new projects, to extend buildings, to refurbish houses or even be given large properties to run by trusts or Local Authorities, but more often than not it is exceptionally hard to raise finance continually for the day-to-day running costs of such projects. From my experience and studies I have been amazed at how quickly funds have been raised for buildings or refurbishment. With one project in particular, I saw a million pounds come in within a few days, yet within twelve months the project had no finance available for the day-to-day running. Even within my own projects we have raised £55,000 required in less than three months, but we struggle from day to day to meet financial needs. Also over the past few years we have seen large established Christian organisations making staff redundant due to a lack of funding.

All of these pitfalls must be realistically taken into consideration when setting up projects. Projects working out of well-established churches or organisations, such as the Church of England, Baptist churches, Pioneer and others with an existing infrastructure with accountability, have more chance of succeeding than one or two individuals attempting to set up a project without the support of any such organisation.

In setting up a project we must be aware that as a country we are now part of the EC and may find ourselves coming under European legislation (dealt with in depth in a later chapter). Within the UK and Ireland, where much of my work takes place, I am aware that there are many different cultures and settings as well as various groupings. For Christians it is important that we respect the culture and value base of the regions people live in. If a project is successfully working in the south of England it does not necessarily mean it will work in Birmingham or Wales. I was once sitting on a Board of Christian counsellors and stated that we were to initiate a counselling course in the Welsh language for Welsh-speaking churches. A large number found this highly amusing and this upset me greatly. I realised, possibly for the first time, that I was not English and felt discriminated against by a group I greatly respected. We were able to deal with this before the wound became too deep or a rift developed. As a non-Welsh-speaking Welshman, I found myself defending the language and was thereby made more aware of the diversity of understanding of various cultures within the UK. (As it turned out the course was highly successful and Welsh-speaking Christians are receiving help and support through this medium.)

Another problem that often arises is in our 'special relationship' with the United States of America. Although we may speak the same language, the cultural differences between the UK and the USA are quite wide. The American culture is seen as an adolescent culture or a therapeutic society very often demanding constant change. If we try to integrate much of what works well in the USA, we very often find it does not work well here, with projects based on American systems often lasting only between three and five years. Part of the reason for this is the differences in the caring infrastructure and the accepted financial systems in the two countries. The culture of the US accepts that the majority of its services have to be paid for. Analysts and researchers have stated that American people pay fairly large sums of money into insurance policies from birth to the grave, and therefore they expect to have the best service or provision on tap, which includes therapy and counselling. Only recently was it discovered, when financial houses had to cut back due to lack of investment, that there was no evidence that much of the therapy and counselling being offered by secular and professional society actually worked. There is a danger that within both the pastoral and community settings we could take on an American-type system which implies that everyone who has difficulties needs therapy or counselling.

As I look at the whole counselling scene developing with a bias towards the American model, I sometimes feel that it is the therapists who keep putting the money in just to keep the merry-go-round going rather than the system being for the benefit of the client. So the counsellor needs counselling and supervision, the supervisor needs supervision and therapy, and the therapist needs therapy and more therapy to meet the needs of the supervisor and counsellor. In our quest for care and counselling we could well find that the needs of therapists and counsellors outweigh those of the client, thus creating a co-dependency system or parasitic relationships within the working counselling environment. I have no doubt that counselling, pastoral care and biblical ministry will be a growth industry well into the next century, but accrediting bodies should be aware of the differences in culture existing in the UK and be prepared to take off their blinkers to prevent them from becoming a closed intro- verted body. As a professional with over twenty-five years' experience of working with people as a counsel- lor, minister and trainer, I firmly believe in the need for good practice within the church and the community, and in the need to reach out to the community with an aware- ness of local needs and culture.

I

Counselling within the Pastoral Church Setting

In setting up counselling in the church it is essential that clear boundaries are established. This will include the service that is being offered and a clear definition between counselling and ministry. The Christian counsellor will very often use prayer and Scripture as part of their counselling practice. Although some secular counsellors may find this a problem, it is one of the foundation stones of counselling within the Christian setting. It is important that the church and counsellors working in that environment clearly state the service they are offering and always seek permission before praying with a client. The church is a rich tapestry of colours, designs and stitches, and it is of paramount importance that suitable management structures exist ensuring accountability of all those who work within them, particularly those involved in pastoral care, counselling and ministry.

In many cases the counselling teams will be accountable to the pastor, leader or appointed person and therefore will be required to work within a framework or structure laid down. Some Christians find it difficult to work within the church setting and to be accountable to structure, supervision, a code of ethics and ongoing training. They may feel that because they are 'called of God' to counsel, they do not need any form of supervision or accountability. The Association of Christian Counsellors has laid down excellent guidelines and standards for those working in the church setting and has a statement of faith, a code of

17

ethics, standards for supervision, recommendations for ongoing training and a value base in counselling which supports those in the pastoral Christian setting. As there has been a growth in counselling over the last ten years in this setting, some tension has been caused in the process of setting up standards. This tension exists both within the church and secular society, where there is a sense of not wanting Christians to be involved in counselling. I have found this is generally due to ignorance. For example, in discussions with secular counsellors and training agencies about the work of the Association of Christian Counsellors, I have found that statements are made without any knowledge of the standards being set. This often surprises me as these people use the word 'professional' in their code of ethics and work, yet they are very unprofessional and closed in the statements they make. My prayer is that we will see closer working links between the Christian accrediting bodies, the church and those working in the secular field.

Why the need for counselling?

Many pastors and leaders within the church setting have discussed with me areas in which they are finding difficulties in dealing with problems brought to them by their congregation. They have stated that they feel ill-equipped to counsel, as the issues arising are far beyond their own personal experience or training. They wish to help the members of their congregations through their life journeys and often suggest that they consider seeing a counsellor or therapist outside the church setting. Some have reacted badly to this and have said that they would not see a secular counsellor or therapist because of different value bases being presented and have asked to see Christian counsellors. I would not agree with many of the statements being made by Christian counsellors about secular workers, yet I can understand the way people think, especially where language is not clearly defined or jargon is used such as 'evangelical' or 'person-centred'.

Within our present church setting we are having to deal with all of the problems experienced in society. This includes the increasing number of people going through divorce, child abuse issues, nervous breakdowns and depression, unemployment, stress, family issues and the break up of the nuclear family. When pastoring a church some twenty years ago, the majority of these problems would have been dealt with in the family or extended family, but we are discovering more people from the community are turning to the church for help and support. It is also interesting to see that these problems are arising in all Christian denominations and new churches. I have often been amazed as a counsellor at how many clients from churches that do not believe in counselling, openly preach against it and write books in that vein, who have come to see me with major situations in their lives. I have been greatly encouraged in my role as Director of a training organisation by the number of church leaders and members who are now applying for training.

Definitions of counselling

Counselling can be defined as 'that activity which seeks to help people towards constructive change in any or every aspect of their lives through a caring relationship and within agreed boundaries'.

Each counselling methodology comprises *assumptions*, *aims* and *methods*. The assumptive basis and overall aims may be implicit or explicit.

Counselling which is distinctively Christian can be defined as 'that activity which seeks to help people towards constructive change in any or every aspect of their lives through a caring relationship and within agreed boundaries, but with all the assumptions, aims and methods undergirded by Christian commitment, insight and values'.

(*Taken from ACC Statement of Faith*)

The uniqueness of Christian counselling

Whether the counsellor is a minister, psychologist, psychiatrist or social worker, certain principles make Christian counselling unique. (The following are taken from Meier, Minirth, Wichern and Ratcliffe, *An Introduction to Psychology and Counselling*, Monarch 1994.)

First, Christian counselling accepts the Bible as the ultimate source of standards. Christians are not left to be 'tossed back and forth', but can look to a final authority. Relying on the Holy Spirit to guide them through the Bible, Christians are not dependent on their own consciences to direct their behaviour. If conscience agrees with the word of God, it is valid; if not, conscience is invalid. The Bible not only gives insights into human behaviour but also puts everything into proper perspective. It tells who we are, where we came from, our nature and purpose.

Second, Christian counselling is unique because it depends on not only the human will to be responsible, but also on the enabling indwelling power of the Holy Spirit to conquer human problems. Although all of us are responsible for our own actions, we sometimes choose irresponsibly. Through God's power, however, we no longer need to be slaves to a weak will, our past environment or social situations. Although problems do not disappear when we accept Christ, we gain new power to deal with them. Although by nature human beings are selfish and tend to ignore or hate God (Romans 1:28–32), Christians through faith receive the Spirit, who gives them victory in overpowering their sinful nature.

Third, Christian counselling is unique because it effectively deals with the counsellee's past. Many traditional personality theories (particularly psychoanalytic theories) deal exclusively with the past. Because Christians find themselves forgiven for past events, they can be guilt-free (1 John 1:9) and look forward to the future (Philippians 3:13–14). Even if some past events require insight and specific prayer to remove resentment and bitterness, believers have a secure position in Christ.

Fourth, Christian counselling is unique because it is based on God's love. God loves us (1 John 4:10) and as his love flows through us we love others and care for them (Romans 12:9–21). A Christian counsellor feels a spiritual affinity with other Christians and helps them to grow in Christ as they solve their problems.

Fifth, Christian counselling is unique because it deals with the whole person. The Christian counsellor is aware that the physical, psychological and spiritual aspects of human beings are intricately related.

Setting the scene

At present there is no requirement for counsellors in the church setting to be accredited, but this is being looked at by various groups throughout Europe. It is unlikely that this situation will change for some time due to the existing confusion on standards in secular society. I have been working with the National Vocational Qualifications Lead Body for Advice, Guidance and Psychotherapy and other professional bodies including the Association of Christian Counsellors, and I can see it is going to take some time before standards are clearly defined. However, I firmly believe that there is a need for those counselling within the pastoral church setting to be offering a clearly defined service which should have the following:

(a) Trained counsellors
(b) Trained supervisors
(c) Management board/leadership team
(d) Literature
(e) Code of ethics
(f) Complaints procedure
(g) Contracts
(h) Indemnity cover
(i) Membership of an accrediting body (ACC, BAC or other).

Setting up a counselling team (see also Appendix A and A (i))

In a church setting it is advisable that the pastor or main elders do not lead the counselling group. Where possible it should be an individual who has a calling on their life in this area and is clear about the direction in which God is leading them. The counselling team leader needs to be trained, under supervision and a member of an accrediting body, working with responsibility to the pastor/elders/minister.

Included in the pastoral setting will be the local or wider church, para-church organisations, Christian residential centres and Christian counsellors who work privately with accountability to the church. In the pastoral setting Christian assumptions and aims will usually be explicit.

It is important to remember that counselling in the pastoral setting is essentially an aspect of Christian caring within the mutual ministry of the body of Christ. With this understanding, accountability can be seen to be furthered by recognised training programmes in Christian contexts, along with supervision and accreditation.

Aims of a counselling team

These should be clearly set out, taking into account the following questions:

1. What work do we intend to do?
2. Are we going to work with Christians only?
3. Are we going to work in a wholeness or healing type ministry?
4. Are we going to offer general counselling in an appropriate sensitive non-directive manner?
5. Do we see ourselves in pastoral or community counselling?

If a team is working in a church setting, the counsellees will be mainly Christians or individuals and families who come to the church and ask for help.

It is advised that the church provides a financial budget for the counselling work and that its team be trained and supported by groups within the church and other training agencies. Regarding support, it is recommended that an outside counsellor/advisor be available to team members. The counsellor/advisor needs to be trained, under supervision and a member of an accrediting body. The planning team should be aware that there is a danger of the counselling ministry taking over the central role of the church. In some circumstances it will be unavoidable and a church will feel it is appropriate for its leadership to head up the counselling team.

Functions of a counselling team

When setting up a counselling service within the church the team should spend much time in prayer, seeking God on the way forward and how they intend to function as a group. This may also require the setting up of a steering group. Later some of this group should become a permanent board. The steering group or board ought to consider the following:

1. What is it going to cost?
2. How much time should we give?
3. From where are we going to operate?
4. What extra support do we need?
5. Who can be appointed to lead the team?
6. What literature or advertising materials are required?

In setting out the function, make sure the following points are covered:

1. The work and purpose of the group must be clearly defined, with a specified target area.
2. A decision needs to be made as to how often the group meets and who calls the meeting.
3. The group should be set up either on a permanent or short-term basis, and if short term the length of time given. A review date could be considered.
4. Financial requirements must be stated.

It is important to keep in mind that a team targeting to work with single parents will function differently from a team working with AIDS sufferers. Although there will be similarities in these two areas of need, there will be major differences. In the majority of cases there will be a third party involved. Clearly defined aims are important.

Team members

Team members must have relevant training and/or experience, and a good Christian counsellor is a realist not a dreamer. The demands are enormous and therefore can create tremendous strains and pressures, so it is important that support systems are built in from the beginning to care for and supervise all team members. Where people do not have any training or experience but have caught the vision for the project, they should be encouraged to seek the necessary training. This will apply to those who will deal with the administration, as well as to the counsellors.

It is vital that team members have outside consultancy support that does not come from their own church or management group. It is recommended that a consultant be asked to join the team in an advisory capacity. This person should be someone who is respected in the Christian field and prepared to give advice. There are dangers in team members trying to counsel one another – it is much more constructive for them to seek counsel from their outside consultant or other suitable experienced counsellor.

Counsellors should have varying backgrounds, training and life experience, and be both male and female. Where possible in a team concept, the directors/managers/co-ordinators should comprise a male and a female working in joint posts, even if this is a voluntary situation.

It is not advisable to work alone, especially in an empty building or other setting where there are no people available for back up. Ideally, there should be two, possibly three, counsellors present in a session; in the majority of cases this will be acceptable to the counsellee. Also it protects the counsellors from any accusations that could be brought against them at a later date. The team should not attempt cross-gender counselling, ie a male should not counsel a female or vice versa. (For suggested team structure see Appendix B.)

The counselling environment

The environment where counselling takes place should be conducive to both counsellor and client. I am sure we have all visited hospitals, social work departments, educational centres and counselling centres within both community and pastoral settings and been appalled by the unsuitability of the setting. For churches setting up a counselling service it is important that time is invested in looking at the environment in which they intend to work. Where the church is working with a small number of individuals, a quiet area will be needed, with suitable rooms which are well ventilated and well lit, with appropriate furnishing, easily accessible toilets, tea- and coffee-making facilities, and where possible a separate entrance. Where a larger counselling service is being planned, a small waiting area will be needed, with reading material, toilets and possibly a receptionist, and two or three counselling rooms tastefully decorated and furnished with adequate sound-proofing. Literature describing the service on offer should be available in all rooms. (See Appendix C.)

Contracts

Within the pastoral setting it is advisable to have contracts between:

1. Client and counsellor
2. Counsellor and supervisor
3. Counsellor, supervisor and church
4. Other agencies and the church.

It is essential that all those who work within a pastoral setting realise that we do not always have all the answers and that with the client's permission there may be need to refer on to another agency, Christian or secular, that is better equipped to help the individual with their problems. (See Appendices D and D(i).)

Confidentiality

Clear guidelines concerning confidentiality are as essential in the pastoral setting as they are in every other counselling setting. Guidelines given by the Association of Christian Counsellors and the British Association of Counsellors provide good examples. In the area of confidentiality it is important that the client realises the counsellor is under supervision and accountable to a ministry team or board, and that if a serious crime has taken place – especially with regard to children – they may find themselves in a position where counselling has to cease. It should be stated in the literature if there are areas in which you do not counsel, so that potential clients are aware of this. Also those working in the pastoral setting who are employed by statutory bodies or Health Trusts may have a conflict of interests with regard to their employment, eg a social worker may be counselling a client who is not aware that the counsellor is a social worker and may raise an issue such as child abuse. The counsellor then informs the client he/she is a social worker, resulting in conflict for both parties. I am aware of such situations and have been called in as advocate or consultant. These situations could have been avoided if the client was informed of the occupation of the counsellor at the outset of counselling.

For a list of possible counselling issues that could be encountered see Appendices E, E(i) and E(ii).

2

Counselling in the Community

Over the past ten years we have seen a number of Christian counselling centres opening across the country working within the church and community. These have been set up by trusts and in the majority of cases work very closely with statutory bodies, voluntary organisations, Health Trusts and other community organisations. Such centres will be working in a much larger environment and could well be counselling centres in a town or community offering residential or day care, and counselling. Generally they will be working from a Christian value base and will be called Christian counselling centres, often with a name before, like my own Barnabas Christian Counselling Centre. It is important for these centres to be clear in dealing with clients and referrals as to the service they offer, clearly stating they are a Christian organisation so that there are no hidden agendas. I realise that in some cases there could be discrimination due to the use of the word 'Christian', just as there can be with Hindu or Muslim. A 'Christian' ethos is no longer acceptable to all sections of society. I have also discovered that some other professional bodies will not work with the Association of Christian Counsellors due to its statement of faith. This is regrettable, but perhaps an inevitable consequence of our being open in all our dealings.

The community setting includes the local and wider community, the caring professions, secular counselling organisations, institutions and residential centres, as well as other statutory and voluntary organisations also with accountability to the community, and the Christian counsellor who works privately. In the community setting the Christian counsellor will use his/her faith and value base implicitly.

Christian counsellors who work within the wider community may operate in two ways. First, they may work in an overtly Christian service to which non-believers come realising that the counselling on offer is Christian. This type of counselling could be seen as a Christian work operating on the 'light principle', where Christian counselling and help are offered to the community with a clear contract between client and counsellor that Christian counselling will be practised.

Second, Christians may also work within the community (eg, in the Social Services, medical practice and other secular organisations) where they will counsel all who come, alongside counsellors trained in secular counselling methods. This could be seen as Christians working according to the 'salt principle'. Here the contract between client and counsellor is not Christian, but the counsellor none the less works within a personal Christian framework while acting within the secular system.

Professional team

Christians working in a community setting will need to look at the whole aspect of professionalism. Generally, a group will be working with professional agencies or individual doctors, health visitors, social workers, teachers, psychiatrists, etc., who will expect professional attitudes. Sadly Christians can sometimes be a little arrogant and ignore some of the very good work being done in the secular field. There are people achieving good results in both secular society and the church. Counselling teams should prayerfully consider their involvement in the wider community and with professional agencies. It is important to understand the network and language used by professional agencies. It is highly recommended that a counselling team should include one member who is qualified in a relevant profession. This person should not be expected to work as a counsellor, but be available to the team for advice and support.

It is well worth considering what terms of reference are to be used when setting up a trust or counselling agency. Terms of reference lay down boundaries on the areas of work you intend to be involved in. It may also be worth appointing a member of the team to research professional and charitable agencies and make a record of what is available for current and future use. This will highlight areas where work is already being done so that people can be referred and duplication can be avoided. Statutory and charitable bodies usually hold general meetings once a quarter, and a community counselling team ought to be represented on as many as possible to give the project a profile in the community and keep up to date with what the other bodies are doing.

Setting up an agency for community counselling

When the team and its role is confirmed, inform outside agencies by giving them the following details:

1. Qualifications and experience of team members.
2. Service and support you can offer. This should include services you are able to offer in times of disaster or family tragedy.
3. The types of referrals you are prepared to take. (Be very

clear as to whether you intend to encourage clients to attend your church or become committed Christians.)

4. If you have a general purpose, for example, giving support, care, love and counsel, this too should be stated clearly. (It has been found that people who are being counselled in general areas will very often come to church through experiencing Christian love and support.)

See Appendix F for agencies with which a community based project could be working.

See Appendix G for setting up a Christian counselling agency in the community.

There are several different options as to the way a centre is set up. This could be a registered charity, a non-profit-making limited company, or a business linked to a church or Christian organisation. It is advisable when setting up such projects that specialists such as lawyers, accountants, architects, consultant counsellors and those skilled in completing feasibility studies are called in to give advice. When setting up projects many people feel that money spent in this area is wasted because there is little or no immediate return, but my experience has taught me the importance of using specialists for guidance. Also indemnity cover is an essential component in setting up a centre. The organisation should be a member of a professional body like the British Association of Counsellors or Association of Christian Counsellors.

Clearly defined aims are important: if the group is set up to work in the community in general, it will be able to help in all areas, but if it is a specialist unit for single parents, the aims of the group will not be able to meet the requirements of, say, an individual or family with AIDS.

Venue

The team should take their time in selecting the venue, and realistic funds will have to be made available, keeping in mind ongoing running costs as well as purchase price and refurbishment. Again I would emphasise the need to employ the services of a surveyor and an accountant. Counselling can be a very expensive ministry and many thousands of pounds may be required to set up an office of a suitable standard. It is important to work out a meaningful budget, even if it takes time to bring the agency to its full potential. Do not necessarily select the first building you see – look around. Talk to doctors, health authorities, solicitors, etc. They may let you use an empty room on their premises and allow you to decorate or convert on a lease basis. In some cases you will find that if you are prepared to acquire a building and carry out renovation on a five-year lease, the offices may be given to you free of charge for the period of use. Make sure that the venue you have is decorated to the highest possible standard. If finances are not available, you may have to find a temporary venue for the first few months. This may even be your own home – although it is not recommended.

The venue must be carefully selected, just as in the pastoral setting. As previously stated, it should be suitable in size, location and accessibility, according to the type of centre envisaged. As in the pastoral setting, a waiting area and toilets are essential, as are an appropriate number of counselling rooms, which should be sound-proofed. Make the counselling rooms comfortable, with tasteful decoration and carpets, good seating arrangements, tea- and coffee-making facilities, suitable ventilation and heating, carefully chosen lighting and a few plants and pictures. There shouldn't be any distractions. Make sure your premises are accessible by public transport, and they are clearly signposted. Remember that premises which require climbing more than one flight of stairs may cause problems for some people.

From time to time there may be a need for residential care or family support for counsellees. It is not advisable to take them into your own home. Try to arrange a network of homes through the churches in your area, or make contact with organisations such as CARE, which have a list of homes available for people. If setting up any form of residential care, keep in mind that this is extremely expensive, especially if it involves counsellees who are not entitled to state benefits (apart from exceptional cases, the only allowance for which they may qualify is housing benefit). Such matters need to be treated with caution.

Finance

The agency must keep in mind that there are going to be costs incurred. These can be large or small according to the overall vision for the work. We must always be honest when handling other people's money and state clearly how finances are being used. If you are charging for this service, state that you are charging, with costs clearly written down. If your work is a faith work, always give a receipt for gifts and have cheques made out to the name of your group. Never accept finance unless a receipt is given. If a person refuses to accept a receipt, it is advisable to make one out anyway and keep it on file. Always bank money immediately and keep a record of amounts given and by whom. People can be very generous and will want to bless you and your organisation, but they have a right to know details of how their money is being spent. Make sure that your books are always up to date and a yearly financial statement is made available. It is always best to use an accredited accountant who is not part of your group or church setting, therefore avoiding a conflict of interest.

There are many advantages in being a registered charity, not least of all the tax repaid from covenants and gifts. In setting up the team, it is always worthwhile considering covenanted giving from your group as early as possible. If it is decided to set up as a registered charity it is most important to get all the relevant Charity Commission information regarding how to operate accounts and make claims.

Confidentiality

This area has been touched upon in the pastoral section but it is so important that it needs repeating. The boundaries of confidentiality must be set up by the organisation from the start and all who work there must agree to keep to these. This could be backed up within the contract. The clients should also have the boundaries of confidentiality explained to them verbally and in writing, again with a clause in the contract between client and counsellor. The organisation needs to be fully aware of the legal position and confidentiality where a crime is disclosed, be it active or past. Anybody who works within the project must be aware of the need for confidentiality. This includes any administration staff and especially those who arrange appointments. Confidentiality equally applies to the handling and storing of records. Ideally any details of counselling, referrals, letters from potential clients, and counselling notes should be handled by as few people as possible and be stored under lock and key. (See also Chapter 4.)

3

Caring and Counselling in a Church Context

Over the past twenty-five years we have seen major changes in what is known as the 'established' church, the evangelical church and the new church movement. The church has always been involved in care and counselling, but within the last decade or so people have begun to speak openly about problems and issues. In many cases we are no longer sitting in pews looking at the backs of other people's heads, but tend to be more involved in relationships. We share open discussions in house groups, dealing with real-life issues and these enable individuals to cope in their spiritual walk and family life. However, while encouraging people to be more open and discuss real issues, many have not been prepared or equipped to deal with the immensity of the problems that have come to light. These have included issues of child abuse, marital and family breakdowns, depression, stress, anorexia and homosexuality. As the church has begun to look at these issues many pastors, leaders and church workers have sought training in counselling, care and specific specialist areas. In doing so this has created a problem for some church leaders where they have found themselves involved in the professional side of counselling and on occasions the insistence by some people that all problems that arise need to be counselled. This has caused tension between leadership, counsellor and congregation.

In exploring this area there are some important guidelines for those involved in leadership, pastoral care and counselling. *The fundamental role of the church is to preach the gospel* – counselling and all other ministries follow. At all times church leaders are responsible for the welfare of their congregation and therefore counsellors and carers need to be accountable to their church leadership.

In counselling, confidentiality is important, but in the church setting the pastor/church leader will need to be made aware, with the counsellee's consent, that they are receiving counselling. Sometimes it is better not to counsel in the church setting and it should be recommended that the counsellee see a counsellor outside of the church setting. Before any counselling begins all counsellees need to be made aware that the pastor/church leader will be told of the counselling as a matter of church policy. Within the pastoral setting there is a great need for discernment in counselling as some people may require ministry such as prayer, healing or other spiritual input alongside the counselling, or even instead of it. This is one of the main reasons why church leadership, ministry team leaders or an appropriate appointed person should be involved with the counselling team. No counsellor should counsel within the church setting without the knowledge and agreement of the church leadership.

Looking into the area of training, the question is often posed: 'Do all those involved in church-based counselling need to be trained to the highest level?' My answer is 'no'. There is a need for basic training to equip skilled listeners, carers and helpers, but there is also a danger that we could produce all-singing, all-dancing, all-trained and accredited counsellors to whom people are afraid to go as they are seen as too professional and unapproachable. The majority of problems that occur in people's lives are issues such as loneliness, family stresses, marriage difficulties, spiritual questions and everyday stress-related difficulties that can be satisfactorily resolved by someone who will listen, maybe over coffee and a bun, pray with them and befriend them. Trained and accredited Christian counsellors working under supervision could be available where deeper problems come to light needing greater and more specific expertise. Not all the problems we deal with in the church involve abuse or marriage breakdown. Some are everyday life issues that church leaders, congregation and house groups can help people work through with a strategy of care and support.

From time to time there will be major issues which trained counsellors and the leadership team may not be able to deal with, and it is important that referring on to an appropriate caring or counselling centre be seriously considered. If this does happen the church will still need to work alongside in a supportive capacity.

It is most important that those who are chosen to lead counselling and caring groups within churches are carefully and prayerfully chosen, looking at character as well as aptitude, training and availability. Training and availability do not necessarily provide the equipment to lead a team, and a counselling team leader also needs to have the necessary characteristics which encourage the team to work in harmony with mutual respect for each other's abilities and shortcomings, and in balance with the other ministries of the church.

The problems of a church-based counselling team are different from those of teams based in the community, but there is equal potential successfully to help individuals improve their lifestyle and experience and help them move from a place of need to a place of being able to cope. The church has a resource of people helpers which, with a little training, guidance, good leadership and a lot of prayer, can be most effective in helping people achieve a balanced godly view of life.

Those who become involved in the church counselling or caring team will need special training in the area of boundaries relating to church activities. It is important to know which 'hat' you are wearing to avoid impromptu counselling sessions at the end of church meetings or house groups. Issues for counselling should be kept strictly to counselling appointments. The counsellor has to be the one who ensures this happens, by setting and keeping to the boundaries. If a counsellee seeks help outside of an appointment this can be effectively handled by suggesting they write the issue down and bring it to the next scheduled appointment; it will be the first thing you explore together then. In this way the counsellor is neither dismissing the counsellee nor breaking agreed boundaries. This strategy prevents every church meeting or house group becoming another counselling session.

Counsellors working in the church should only take on clients who come to them through the proper channels set down by the church leadership. Anyone approaching them direct should be advised of the appropriate procedure.

Due to the different relationships that exist within the church the setting up of a counselling team may seem to be fraught with pitfalls, but it is important that the church is willing and equipped to help its own in the same way that it should be equipped and prepared to evangelise.

4

Common Ground for Pastoral- and Community-Based Counselling Centres

In both the pastoral and community setting there are common guidelines which need to be followed, whether the project is day or residential care, or counselling.

Once the infrastructure of the counselling centre, be it pastoral or community based, is in place, lines of accountability are clearly stated and provision for training for all team members is made, it is essential that boundaries in the counselling relationship are clearly defined. The infrastructure should also include professional indemnity cover, all necessary insurance, financial budget and audit cycle.

Contracts

Contracts are a fairly new concept for many people, and although they have been around in social work counselling and supervision for some time, they are often not kept. The first contract that should be set is the contract of employment or voluntary contract between the board or trust and the counsellor. The contract should clearly define the expected role of the counsellor in the work of the trust or organisation. These contracts should be regularly reviewed as part of ongoing supervision and audit cycle. This review should take place separate from client-based supervision and should be part of the managerial duties of the board or trust.

The next contract should be set between the counsellor and the client. This contract should clearly define the counselling process and the service being given, the time and venue of counselling, the number of sessions before review, note-taking and confidentiality, and the cost of each session, if applicable. Ideally this contract should cover six appointments plus a review. If after a review further counselling is agreed, another six-week contract should be set up and so on, according to need. This method is preferred by professional organisations, especially fund-holding organisations that charge for the service. It also gives the counsellor and client an opportunity to take stock of the work so far. A break of at least one appointment at this stage is useful in order to assess the need or otherwise for ongoing work, or maybe a need for referral to another more appropriate source of help.

The next contract is that between the counsellor and the supervisor. This should set out formal supervision with agreed times and agendas, confidentiality, number of hours the counsellor sees the supervisor, and fee if applicable. If you are working within an agency the supervision should be provided both internally and externally for all levels of staff and counsellors.

Contracts between the agency and Health Trusts are relatively new within the field of counselling, and fund-holding trusts are continually assessing the outcome in the service they are paying for with their clients. Such contracts should clearly state the service you are offering, an agreed number of sessions, the method of payment (contractual or one off), personal indemnity cover of agency/counsellors, accrediting body, confidentiality and referrals.

See Appendices D and D(i).

Fees

The issue of whether or not counselling projects should make a charge for their services is a subject of much debate. One of the major factors is how the project is financed. Many church-based projects do not charge as it is seen as a service of the church. Others argue that people put higher value on something they pay for and would take counselling more seriously and work towards change more readily if a fee was involved. The final decision obviously has to be made by those who are setting up the project according to the criteria agreed upon. Where there are overheads to be covered, including the maintenance and running of a centre, staff salaries, etc, charging for counselling may be a necessity. A sliding scale of charges to suit the income of the client is often an effective solution. If the decision is made to charge for counselling this must be very clearly stated on all literature and also whether or not these fees are negotiable. Some organisations do not charge for counselling itself but ask for an administration fee for the initial appointment. For some this has cut down the number of people who make appointments and do not keep them.

Where residential accommodation is included, a fee for the accommodation should be considered. The ongoing costs of these projects can be phenomenal and unless there is a great deal of guaranteed committed financial support, a scale of charges will be necessary. This needs to be looked at realistically as raising funds for the day-to-day running of projects is one of the most difficult parts of keeping a project going. A bursary fund may also be considered for those who cannot afford to pay but would benefit from the service. It is not unreasonable to ask the referring agency for help towards the finance for the client if the potential client cannot afford it themselves, especially where the referring agency is a statutory body, Health Trust or church.

Team-building

Effective working teams do not just happen, they evolve from good planning, good communication, training and time. A key ingredient is mutual respect at all levels.

Procedure manuals may also be a good way of maintaining a team. If everyone carries out the same procedures within the office, such as when dealing with referrals, counselling, record-keeping and referring on, it enhances the smooth running of the service provided. This helps to ensure that everyone is working to achieve a high standard of consistent good service. Clear identification of roles, where possible, can also help, and it is useful if individuals within the team know early on who they can speak to if they are not happy with the procedure or another team member. It is to be hoped that within a team of Christians misunderstandings or disagreements can be resolved quickly, and ideally good lines of communication will be established before they happen.

Teams are also built by members spending time together in the initial stages, sharing how they see things developing, their vision for the project and themselves. This can help to avoid people having hidden agendas for the future or unrealistic expectations. Team meetings and training days should be part of the programme for the project from the beginning. Working through some personality tests together could be a useful tool, and the Myers Briggs is just one you could consider. It may help to avoid developing a team that is imbalanced and therefore lacking in some areas.

Frequent, planned team meetings will provide the opportunity to iron out misunderstandings or anxieties. It is important to keep in mind that a team involved in caring for others needs to be cared for, and provision needs to be made for this. It is not unusual for counsellors or carers to come across unresolved issues in their own lives as they train or while they are counselling others. Access to help outside the immediate group should therefore be available.

Indemnity cover

This has already been mentioned in passing and is another essential item for the protection of counsellors and clients alike. At present the cost of cover is relatively low because very few cases involving counselling have gone to court. If you belong to a professional agency such as ACC or BAC, it may be possible to arrange preferential rates with some insurance companies. Counselling within the church may already be covered by existing church insurance, but this most definitely needs to be checked out.

Record-keeping

Before any counselling begins it is necessary to have established guidelines on record-keeping for all counsellors. This will include the whole process from initial referral to completing a contract of counselling, as well as notes taken during a counselling session. It is important to bear in mind that clients have a right to see all that is written about them and then to keep the notes when the counselling is complete. Obviously confidentiality will be a key issue throughout. A storage system that keeps names and addresses separate from session notes will be needed, with a coded system to match them if necessary. All counsellors will need to be aware of this. The records should then be kept under lock and key with only limited access. It should be decided how long notes are to be kept after counselling ends and how they will be destroyed safely after this. A shredding machine may well be the answer.

Counsellors should be aware of the necessity of writing up case studies for accreditation purposes and of keeping their own counselling log containing time, date and venue of session, a client code and a very brief description of the session (two or three lines). Supervision logs will also need to be kept by the counsellors. Some guidance on keeping counselling and supervision logs should be part of the training.

Where there is no office to keep counselling files in safety, individual counsellors may have to be responsible for their own counselling notes. Confidentiality is of the utmost importance and to ensure this a coded system should be used to separate notes from names and addresses. Any client information kept at home must be under lock and key.

Liaising with other agencies

For a counselling agency to have real credibility in the community it cannot exist in isolation but needs to be part of the services offered by the community as a whole. For a Christian counselling service to be accepted, it has to be seen to offer a consistent quality service with high standards of good practice. A willingness to work alongside existing services is essential. Christians often earn themselves a bad name by acting as if they are the only ones with the answers or by appearing on the scene and expecting everyone to be pleased and to use them immediately. The evangelical church is not in competition with other projects being run in the community. Relationships need to be built up with other agencies; they will not just happen. One good way of encouraging this to happen is to let the other services in the community know what you intend to set up once the initial plans have been finalised. You might even make your first contact before this – for example, when you embark on your feasibility study. This first contact is most important and may make the difference between being co-workers in the future or never having further contact. A new project is far more likely to be welcomed if approaches are made in an informed professional manner, with respect for the work already being provided and a willingness to be questioned on the intentions of the new service. As the project progresses and literature is printed, it also helps to send as much information as possible to other local services. A personal visit may prove most productive.

When approaching statutory bodies it is important to bear in mind that there are processes they have to adhere to in different situations. This is especially true when dealing with children. When a client has a child in care or in a possible abuse case, once Social Services are informed there is a set process which cannot easily be stopped. If you are supporting a client where there is Social Service intervention, the fact that you are a Christian counsellor may not be of any importance to them. The procedures of the system have to be allowed for and worked with and not seen as deliberate hindrance to what you are trying to achieve. And it won't help to approach other bodies saying, 'God has told me . . . therefore . . . .'

In setting up any form of centre, whether counselling, residential care or day care, working with drug addicts or alcoholics or any client group, it is a priority that the church has an understanding of the work of the Local Authority, Social Services, Education Department, Health Trusts, voluntary agencies, police and other statutory bodies. One of the best ways to achieve this is to set up a resource pack by writing to your Local Authority for information on services provided.

Major changes took place in April 1996 in Wales and Scotland when the two-tier system of government ceased and District and County Councils disappeared, merging into one body known as a Unitary Authority. This brought together Social Services, formerly run by County Council, with Environmental Health, Planning and Housing, previously run by District Council. Ideally a church- or community-based project should appoint an individual to liaise with these bodies. Information on the organisation/ agency should be available on request. The new Unitary Authorities will also operate in England from a date yet to be confirmed, but these groups are fund-holding and will have finance available for community- and church-based projects. They also have funds available under the 'Village Hall' fund and Community Care Projects. Some fund-holding departments are not always forthcoming with finance to Christian projects and in some cases discriminate against Christian work. Do not become discouraged by this; ask for reasons why funds are not forthcoming. One of the best ways forward for churches working with the Local Authority is to have members of the congregation on the boards of school governors, Health Trusts, Chamber of Trade, etc. This helps to build up a good working relationship within the community.

I would recommend that church groups and those setting up projects be aware of the work of the NSPCC, Barnardo's, The Children's Society, Child Protection Teams and other voluntary and Christian agencies operating in their locality. Before embarking on a project, it is well worth contacting the Home Office, Welsh Office, Scottish Office or Irish Office according to your location for information on the Children Act, the Community Care Act and funding for local projects.

5

Residential Care

Much of my work in Social Services, counselling and the ACC has been in setting up residential and day care and counselling projects in both the Christian and secular setting. I have seen substantial growth in Christian organisations and individuals setting up residential establishments, especially for children, single parents, alcoholics, the homeless and adults with learning difficulties. A number of these have been very successful organisations, such as Teen Challenge, Barnabas House, Living Springs and Promoting Christian Child Care and Action, but in every single case there has been a tremendous personal cost and in many cases a shortfall in finance. I have also seen cases where individuals or groups are called by God to set up projects and may have a clear vision of aims and objectives of the work they would like to do in the caring environment, but have been totally unrealistic in the size of the project. For instance, it may be that a small house or cottage would have sufficed for a day or residential centre – especially in the early stages of the project. Instead the target has been a large mansion or manor house, an old psychiatric hospital or a large disused school. Those concerned have not taken into consideration the sum of money needed for the upkeep of such a property or the number of staff required to man it; nor have they looked at the financial implications of long-term work. As I have said before, it can be relatively easy to raise funds for a building or project in the early stages, but it is another matter to sustain the flow of finance to keep the project going. This is especially so of residential projects. Individuals or groups say that God will provide or that they have faith, and while I may accept this in principle and have experience of this both in my own life and Barnabas House, we can sometimes presume a great deal and act as a result of our own desires or needs.

Recently I was asked to look at a project to care for the homeless and provide training programmes. Some members of the group planning this project said that they had heard from God, while others were uncertain. Some of the uncertainties were due to the size of the proposal (this project would cost £200,000–300,000 prior to opening). I suggested they considered a feasibility study. Half of the group felt this was an excellent idea and realised it would take three to six months to carry out. The rest of the group felt that they were hearing from God and therefore waiting for the results of a feasibility study was totally out of the question. They wanted me to give them an overview of the project that day. I asked the following basic questions:

1. Did they have any finance? (No)
2. Did they believe they would pray in or raise the finance? (Yes)
3. Had they considered the services of an accountant, solicitor and architect to look at the project in some depth? (No)
4. Were they aware of any research data or information on the homeless and their needs in the area? (No)
5. What were the training needs within the area with regard to the project they were setting up? (Not known)

They then asked me to see the building and give my views. The building had been a college, part Dickensian and part modern, with offices and workshops.

Again I posed some basic questions:

1. Had they looked at basic planning permission for change of use? (No)
2. Had they discussed, or were they aware of, building regulations? (No)
3. Had they checked if the unit they intended to use for residential care was suitable regarding fire regulations? (No)

After much discussion my opinion was that the building was not suitable for their needs and renovation would be extremely expensive. In addition, the location of the property was not suitable as the number of homeless in the area was relatively small and well over three-quarters of these would not want to live in or be part of such an environment. Some members of the group were of the opinion that people would travel across the country to stay there. They had not taken into consideration the Community Care Act or considered the possibility of other similar units throughout the UK.

I felt that the building was totally unsuitable for their needs, and the majority of the group agreed. I suggested that they consider a much smaller project after a feasibility study, which could still have the same vision of God's calling but would meet the requirements of the local community and the local church. Unfortunately a small number felt that they needed to go ahead with the project as a separate group, not part of the church vision. They had agreed with the vendor to move into the building prior to purchase while they raised the funds, and they had invested considerable finance, both personal and gifts, into the building. After six months the vendor required the full payment and they believed right up to the last hour, but the finance did not come. This project may have worked quite well in a large inner-city environment or within a catchment area of a number of towns or cities, but unfortunately it was not feasible within the planned location.

I have been deeply saddened over the last five years to see so many Christians investing large sums of money into projects where they have not seriously counted the cost or taken advice. Many have lost their homes and livelihoods. What also interests me is that some of these people are businessmen and women who would not normally go down that road, but because they feel God is speaking they forget the gifts and wisdom they already have. When I ask, 'Who owns the project?' some will say that it is God, but actually they mean themselves.

If a Christian project is to be set up it needs to be defined.

1. If it is a business it should be so called.
2. If it is set up by individuals it should clearly be seen to be so.
3. If it is owned by a church organisation it should be stated.
4. If it is a charity the registered charity number should be included on all literature and correspondence.
5. If it is a non-profit-making limited company the company number should be included on all literature and correspondence.

People setting up a project which is part of a church, charity or non-profit-making charitable body must realise they do not own the project but are only caretakers of all that is invested in the project by others. It is also most important to consult appropriate bodies at the outset if the project may fall into any of the statutory areas for registration. They will give guidance from the planning stage to avoid having to make major alterations to your beautifully reconstructed and decorated property.

When setting up a Christian project take professional advice.

See Appendices H and H(i) for a checklist.

Avoiding pitfalls

When considering the purchase of a building, have a full survey carried out by a chartered surveyor before agreeing to a price. Check with building regulations, and make sure that change of use is possible. Have proper plans drawn up and submitted. Also, consult the Community Care Act, check with the Social Service Inspectorate regarding possible registration, and have outside consultancy advice available.

Do not accept a verbal agreement from any Local Authority body on plans, building regulations or change of use. Check all these with a professional.

This will all cost money but is a good investment.

Catering can be a big issue when considering a residential establishment and can add considerably to financial and manpower needs. Obviously the size and style of the project may be the deciding factor regarding whether your project is to be self-catering or not. A small set-up functioning on a counselling rather than a counselling/caring basis may work very well with the counsellees catering for themselves, especially where the stay is only short and counselling is by appointment. However, a larger therapeutic-type environment may call for full-scale kitchens and catering staff.

All residential provision which comes under the Registered Homes Act 1984 will be inspected twice yearly at minimum by the Registration Authority. The following is taken from a Social Services Policy and Procedure Manual, January 1988, from Dyfed County Council.

8.1 Power of entry and inspection of residential care homes:

Section 17 of the Registered Homes Act 1984 outlines the position with regard to the Authority's power of entry and inspection of residential care homes. The section provides that:

(i) any person authorised by the Secretary of State or by the Registration Authority may at all times enter and inspect any premises that are used, or are believed to be used, as residential care home;

(ii) powers of inspection include the power to inspect any record required to be kept;

(iii) the Secretary of State may require residential care homes to be inspected at such intervals as the Regulations prescribe;

(iv) a person who proposes to exercise any right of entry or inspection shall, if required, produce some duly authenticated document showing his authority to exercise the power;

(v) a person who obstructs the exercise of any such power shall be guilty of an offence.

An inspection carried out under Section 17 can be made at any time of day or night; advance notice does not have to be given.

8.2 Purpose of inspection:

The purposes of inspection have been identified in a variety of publications including Social Services Inspectorate/Department of Health publication entitled 'Inspecting for Quality – Guidance on Practice for Inspection Units in Social Service Departments and other Agencies'. This guidance identifies five main purposes which ensure that:

(i) the quality of users' lives meets agreed standards and both users and staff are protected from abuse, neglect or exploitation;

(ii) appropriate actions are identified to improve performances and standards;

(iii) good practice is promoted and Statutes are complied with;

(iv) service development is promoted via staff recruitment, training and support;

(v) all services are cost effective.

8.3 Formal annual review – inspection procedure:

Currently, for the first annual inspection following registration, a pre-inspection questionnaire is sent to all managers/proprietors three to four weeks before an inspection visit. It is the responsibility of the proprietor or manager to complete and return the pre-inspection questionnaire to the Inspection Unit seven days prior to the agreed inspection date. Detailed in the table below are the areas covered in the first Annual Inspection Report.

Table 1 – Areas Covered in the Annual Inspection Report

1. *Basic information*
   1.1 Name of home
   1.2 Address
   1.3 Proprietor
   1.4 Address if non-resident
   1.5 Number of registered beds
   1.6 Category
   1.7 Registration date
   1.8 Manager, if any
   1.9 Number of residents at time of visit
   1.10 Number of vacancies
   1.11 Number of deaths since last annual report
   1.12 Number of other discharges
   1.13 Date of last full review
   1.14 Number of visits since last review
   1.15 Dates of unannounced visits
   1.16 Matters still requiring attention following previous inspection visits, complaints or reports from Fire Brigade or Environmental Health Department.
2. Residents and their quality of life
3. Health care
4. Menus and meals
5. Premises and facilities
6. Staffing
7. Organisational/Administrative arrangements
8. Management
9. Records
10. Summary/Conclusions.

The format for subsequent annual inspections will involve detailed consideration of matters associated with the quality of care and quality of life for the residents, together with any of the changes taking place within the home.

8.4 Unannounced inspection visits:

As a consequence of the Residential Care Homes Regulations 1988, Authorities are encouraged to place greater emphasis upon unannounced inspection visits.

8.5 Inspection of Local Authority residential care homes:

The National Health Service and Community Care Act 1990 introduced a requirement that Local Authorities inspect their own residential care homes using the same criteria as they apply to the private and voluntary sector.

6

Supervision

Since 1990 the role of the supervisor in the learning situation or work place has come to the forefront. This has come with the introduction of NVQs, SNVQs, the Diploma in Social Work, Counselling in the Work Place and the right of every member of staff or agency to be supervised in the learning process, be it as a student, member of staff or counsellor.

Here are some definitions of 'supervision': 'Supervision is a working alliance between a supervisor and worker or workers in which the workers can reflect on themselves in their working situation by giving an account of their work and receive feedback and, where appropriate, guidance and appraisal. The object of this alliance is to maximise the competence of the worker in providing a helping service' (F. Inskipp and B. Proctor).

'An intensive, interpersonally focused, one-to-one relationship in which one person is designated to facilitate the development of therapeutic competence in the other person' (Loganbill, Hardy and Delworth).

The following paragraph is adapted from Roger Hurding, *Some Theological Reflections on Supervision*.

Christian supervisors are aware that they are men and women called to serve, and that kingdom priorities demand that they do not 'lord it over' their supervisees but rather they seek to serve. This service comprises an influence which, under God, can be normative, formative and restorative. In every dimension of this threefold enterprise – in accountability, confidentiality, example, instruction, one-anotherness and mutuality – there needs to be an awareness not only of the supervisor/supervisee relationship but of the broader contexts. These contexts include most obviously the counsellor/client relationship, but to be more fully biblical, the supervisor should also be mindful of those agencies (local church or counselling organisation) and, indeed, of the wider communities within which the client, counsellor, supervisor and agency all function. Keeping in view this breadth of vision, the Christian supervisor should seek in all these perspectives to be subject to Christ's normative, formative and restorative work in their own lives.

Supervision is an essential part of the ongoing work of any counselling team at all levels and in every setting. The supervisor should be trained in counselling with at least five years' experience and should also have received supervision training. Leadership supervision should come from a peer or outside consultant who can advise, help and support. It is most important that church-based counselling groups make adequate provision for supervision and do not solely rely on God to keep them out of difficulties. God is very good at doing this, but he does ask us all to act responsibly in our calling and I see seeking and providing adequate supervision as doing just this.

The supervisor should have a good working knowledge of the supervisee's level and type of training, the ethos of the church, organisation or project, the models of counselling used and the type of clients being catered for. Ideally the supervision relationship is one that develops over time and has set boundaries, including issues of confidentiality. Supervision should not include counselling for the counsellor. If this becomes necessary someone other than the supervisor should be approached. The supervisors themselves should be involved in regular supervision.

Supervision is part of the criteria for accreditation and can take place in a number of different ways:

1. Individual supervision to assess personal development and give support. This should always take place in a formal manner, not ad hoc.
2. Planned supervision to look at each counsellor's work and arrange help if required, keeping in mind confidentiality.
3. Group supervision in particular tasks or areas of work:
   (a) Individual – one to one.
   (b) Two or more members in an area of work.
   (c) The whole team together.
   (d) Peer supervision.

Supervision needs to be planned with clear tasks in mind, concentrating on members' individual skills and abilities, the group needs and the agency needs.

Formal supervision

This can take the following forms:

1. Formal planned meetings
2. Regular agreed agendas
3. General and/or specific issues
4. Decisions recorded
5. Group or individual.

For formal supervision a contract should be entered into, agreed by supervisor and supervisee. See Appendix I for an example.

Planned supervision is more for support and development. On-the-job coaching and new skills, eg induction and basic skill training.

Informal supervision

This takes the form of demonstration and example as situations occur and is often clarified and confirmed in formal sessions at a later date. There may be unplanned discussions due to crises or situations arising between formal agreed sessions. Space/time may even be created for this purpose.

The amount of supervision required will vary according to the training and experience of the counsellor, the size of the case load and the complexity of cases, but it is advisable for supervision to take place once every four to six weeks for at least an hour. It is also advisable that the supervisee keeps a record of supervision, especially if seeking accreditation. The session time for group supervision will obviously differ according to number.

Supervision is an essential safeguard for both counsellor and client. A good supervisor is trained, experienced and skilled, so the benefit of their services may incur a fee.

See Appendix I(i) for checklist of formal supervision.

7
Training

When considering setting up a counselling centre/service in either the pastoral or community setting, it is most important that training for all those involved is given priority once the boundaries of the service to be offered have been established. This will need to be budgeted for in the financial plan and should be ongoing throughout the life of the project. Careful consideration needs to be given to the type and range of training needed. Office staff as well as counsellors will benefit from both in-house and external training. Working from the base of each individual's existing training and experience, it would be advisable at some point to work out a personal plan for each one involved according to need.

Training in counselling is just as important within the pastoral setting as it is anywhere else. The Holy Spirit is an excellent guide and counsellor, but we do not always 'hear' him correctly or use what we hear in an appropriate manner. I see training as part of our response to God's calling to come alongside those in need so that we learn what is appropriate. Training is part of the equipping enabling us to respond in the most useful way to an individual seeking help. It should also assist in our personal awareness and growth, possibly indicating where adjustment is needed before the counselling role is taken on. We must be aware that we cannot avoid projecting our own hurts and prejudices onto our clients if we have not dealt with them adequately. This is not fair when clients are trying to work through their own hurts. I do not believe counsellors should be permanently in therapy, but they should be open to seek it if the need arises. One of the aims of training should be to highlight strengths and weaknesses so that each counsellor can become aware of the areas of counselling in which they are particularly gifted to work.

A common base of training could be beneficial. If this does not already exist it may be worth considering organising a counselling course for everyone to attend, even if some counsellors have attained a higher level. It is useful for those who work on the administration side to have some counselling knowledge, particularly those who answer the telephone. A telephone answering skills course would be helpful for all who are involved.

The standards and quality of training are important and time needs to be spent on investigating the availability and range of courses. The training background and experience of the trainers, along with their knowledge and experience in training, should also be considered. The courses you choose should be registered/recognised/validated by a professional body and they should be sympathetic to the general ethos of the project.

To equip counsellors to work in a community setting the professionalism of the training should take a high priority. This will help in building up the integrity of the services you are offering with the voluntary and statutory bodies in the area.

It is advisable that all counselling training courses undertaken should be working towards accreditation with a professional body such as the Association of Christian Counsellors or British Association of Counsellors. Information about their requirements for accreditation should therefore be sought at the outset.

Various levels of training are offered by many different

groups and organisations. ACC provides a list of all the training it recognises and this may be helpful. It may be advisable to complete an introductory and advanced course with the same organisation since most courses are designed to follow on from each other. Training from different sources can help to bring variety in models and approach, but it could also cause confusion. If your project intends to specialise in one area, for example pregnancy crisis counselling, it is at this point that specialist training should be sought. Where the intention of the project or church is to provide help over a wide range of counselling issues, individuals could be encouraged to seek specialist training in the areas they are drawn towards or those the project anticipates there being specific need for.

Types of courses

Basic courses

The ACC-recognised basic courses are a minimum of fifty hours and are generally open to anyone with or without previous training or experience in counselling. The particular criteria, timing and course content of the basic course may vary slightly as the individual training organisations holding ACC recognition adhere to a core syllabus but have some freedom in precise details.

The basic course is intended for those who are at the point of considering getting involved in counselling or who already know this is the way God is leading them. It aims to promote high standards of practice in counselling within a recognised framework of accountability and accreditation. Didactic and experiential methods of teaching are used, with the emphasis on group work, pairs and triads so that skills practice and personal awareness are paramount.

The course content includes:

What is counselling?
Counselling models
Skills and qualities of an effective counsellor
Basic listening skills
Communication skills
The process of change
Awareness of self and others
Society and its problems
Importance of supervision
Specific counselling issues
Case studies
Required reading
Home assignments

Advanced courses

Generally these are around 200 hours, again with differences according to the training organisation, but courses with ACC recognition have common criteria and core subjects. Experiential work is key to the course and counselling practice under supervision will be required during the course. The advanced course aims to extend the knowledge and skills base and is open to those who have completed the basic course.

The course content includes:

Counselling models – Christian and secular
Skills and qualities of an effective counsellor
Counselling techniques
Empathy and reflection
Looking at the whole person
The process of change
Self-awareness
Dealing with conflict

Legal issues
Specific counselling issues
Case studies
Role play
Required reading
Home assignments

Specialist courses

These are aimed to cover specific issues which may be types or models of counselling or areas of counselling. They vary in length and method of teaching and are intended to broaden knowledge base and/or skills. Individual organisations may specialise or have a range of specialist courses available.

Supervision training

ACC offers supervision training at four levels. Level one is intended as much for counsellors as supervisors because the content includes fundamentals of what supervision should be.

Training the trainers

This is a specialist course which is aimed at those already involved in course delivery. The course is participative and examines teaching technique, course interaction and presentation skills.

Reading is a useful way of keeping up to date with new thoughts and ideas in counselling as well as looking at areas of counselling not yet covered by training. Journals and other publications can be a useful source of new knowledge. Counsellors at every level should be encouraged to increase their knowledge base by ongoing reading.

See Appendix J for a small selection of suggested reading.

8

Law, Legislation and Code of Ethics

When we are offering any service it is necessary to be aware of all current laws and legislation relating to that service. According to the specific area the project is working with, there is bound to be legislation which has to be taken into account.

Looking at counselling in general there are at present no laws or guidelines as to who can be a counsellor and what training or qualifications they should have. Over the coming years this is expected to change, with the possibility of either a voluntary or statutory code of practice being imposed. This may only apply to those practising in the community setting, but counsellors in every setting should be aiming for high standards of good practice.

The Community Care Act is relevant to many aspects of counselling and support, therefore all centres and projects should have access to a copy and some knowledge of its contents. The Children Act 1989 will also have a bearing on many areas, even when children are not the primary client group. HMSO provide a wide range of readily available publications and leaflets which will be helpful to counsellors, clients and their families, particularly the series of guides aimed at young people and parents. These would be useful resources to many projects.

When considering setting up any type of residential or day centre it is vital to be aware of the possible need for registration with the local Social Services Department and the need for initial and ongoing inspections.

Day care services for the under eights are governed by legislation of the Children Act 1989. Residential services for children of any age are covered by the same Act.

Residential services for adults are covered by the Residential Homes Act 1984, including elderly, mentally infirm, physically handicapped, those with learning difficulties, drug and alcohol abuse and those recovering from mental illness.

Day care services for adults and children over eight may be governed by local guidelines.

The local Social Services Department will need to be contacted for the name of the office required – possibly the Inspection Unit or Quality Assurance Office or similar. Each Local Authority should provide such a department as an independent inspection body for registered services.

Policy and procedure

All organisations need to spend time and effort to ensure that all their policies and procedures are well written in an easy-to-understand style and available for anyone to see. Anti-discrimination is an area which requires particular thought and needs to be part of the good practice of the agency or project. A complaints procedure also needs to be compiled for the internal working of the agency and for counselling again this needs to be clear and available. It is essential that these documents are deemed to be legally acceptable and that consultations regarding their legal status be made with the project solicitor. Everyone working for a counselling agency, whether it is within the church or community setting, needs to have a copy of the anti-discrimination policy and the complaints procedure, and needs to know where to get further copies should they be required.

Anti-discrimination

The Race Relations Act 1976 and the Sex Discrimination Acts 1975 and 1986 make it unlawful to discriminate against individuals on the grounds of their sex, marital status, race, colour, nationality, or ethnic or national origin. It is also unlawful to victimise anyone because they assert or have previously asserted their rights under legislation.

Anti-discrimination may seem a heavy issue for a Christian counselling agency to have to consider, and some may even be of the opinion that Christians would automatically operate in this manner. However, it is important that these issues are seriously considered, particularly when working in the community setting. It is most important that everyone should be on their guard against the danger of allowing preconceptions or stereotypes about capabilities, characteristics and interests of particular groups to influence the treatment of individuals. Such preconceptions may result in discrimination. Although unintentional, this can still have damaging effects, even if it does not give rise to a complaint.

It is important that literature, recruitment, training and working procedures – as well as all interaction with counsellees – are maintained under anti-discrimination guidelines. Once established, these guidelines will need to be kept under review in line with changes in policy and legislation.

Code of ethics

All Christian counselling projects should operate under a statement of faith and a code of ethics. The following comes from the Association of Christian Counsellors and is the accepted basis for counsellors who wish to be members of the ACC.

Statement of Faith and Practice

Basis

The Association affirms the central truths of the Christian faith as expressed in the Bible and in the historic creeds. In particular, it affirms God as Triune, Father, Son and Holy Spirit, and is committed to expressing the lordship of Christ and the authority of Scripture in all areas of belief and practice.

Code of Ethics and Practice

Counsellor/counsellee relationship

Counsellors must take all necessary steps to ensure that the counsellee suffers neither physical nor psychological harm during counselling.

Counsellee autonomy: Counsellors are responsible for working in the ways which promote the counsellee's control over his/her own life and to respect the counsellee's ability to make decisions and change in the light of his/her own beliefs and values.

Counsellors do not normally act on behalf of their counsellees. If they do, it will be at the express request of the counsellee, providing the activity is within the bounds of good practice.

Counsellors must set and monitor boundaries between the counselling relationship and any other kind of relationship, and must make this explicit to the counsellee.

It is absolutely forbidden for counsellors to exploit their counsellees financially, sexually, emotionally or in any other way.

It is constructive and safe to work in pairs, although it is recognised that many counsellors work on their own. If a trainee counsellor is present it should only be with the counsellee's consent.

Records of counselling sessions should normally be kept and the counsellee should be made aware of this. At the counsellee's request, information should be given about the access to these records, their availability to other people and the degree of security with which they are kept. In particular, if a tape or video recording is included, this must not be made without express consent of the counsellee.

Counsellors should be made aware that computer-based records are subject to statutory regulations under the Data Protection Act 1984. From time to time the government introduces changes in regulations concerning the counsellee's right of access to his/her records. Current regulations have implications for counsellors working in Social Services and health care settings.

Counsellors must establish with the counsellees what other counselling and therapeutic help they are receiving. Counsellors should gain the counsellee's permission before conferring with other professionals or church workers.

Exceptional circumstances may arise which give the counsellor good grounds for believing that the counsellee will cause physical harm to others or themselves, or have harm caused to him/her. If this happens the counsellor should make every reasonable effort to persuade the counsellee that a change in agreement about confidentiality is necessary, unless there are grounds for believing the counsellee is no longer able to take responsibility for his/her actions. Whenever possible, the decision to break confidentiality should be agreed between counsellor and counsellee and should be made only after consultation with a counselling supervisor or experienced counsellor.

Counsellors hold different views about whether or not a counsellee's expression of serious suicidal intentions forms sufficient grounds for breaking confidentiality. Counsellors should consider their own views and practice, communicate them to the counsellee and any significant other parties where appropriate. In particular the need to seek medical, legal and supervisory help in the counsellee's interest must be considered.

Christian counsellors need to be particularly aware that the right to confidentiality must not be waived in the context of prayer support and church prayer on the counsellee's behalf without his/her agreement.

Data protection is mentioned in the code of ethic and practice, and is an issue which must be considered when storing any information about individuals on computer. It is important that any organisation looks at the Data Protection Act before it starts setting up data bases of names and addresses, and that it becomes registered if applicable.

Projects dealing specifically with debt counselling may need to be registered. Information and guidance need to be sought if this could apply.

As part of the ongoing work of any type of counselling agency or project it is necessary to have the services of a solicitor. This is an essential element not just in the early stages of a project but throughout its life. In fact it is becoming more important as the number of complaints against counsellors increases. As yet few have ever been brought to court, but as the trends of America reach our shores, bringing the increased tendency to reach for legislation when the outcome is unsatisfactory, it may only be a matter of time before this becomes more commonplace. For the most part, however, a solicitor's role would be one of advisor and safety net. When choosing a solicitor it is important that they have an understanding of the vision of the work and the type of counselling the project is involved in. Their help could also be employed when drawing up contracts of employment for counsellors, clients and other agencies.

Children Act 1989

One of the most important pieces of legislation with regard to families, children and statutory and voluntary agencies is the Children Act 1989. The following is a glossary of terms contained within the Act.

Accommodation: Being provided with accommodation replaces the old voluntary care concept. It refers to a service that the Local Authority provides for the parents of children in need, and the children themselves. The child is not in care when she/he is being provided with accommodation; nevertheless the Local Authority has a number of duties towards children for whom it is providing accommodation, including the duty to discover the child's wishes regarding the provision of accommodation and to give them proper consideration. [s20]

Adoption: The total transfer of parental responsibility from the child's natural parents to the adopter/s.

Affidavit: A statement in writing and on oath sworn before a person who has the authority to administer it, eg a solicitor.

Appeal: An appeal in care proceedings will now be heard by the High Court or, where applicable, the Court of Appeal. All parties to the proceedings will have equal rights of appeal. On hearing an appeal, the High Court can make such orders as may be necessary to give effect to its decision. [s94]

Area Child Protection Committee (ACPC): Based upon the boundaries of the Local Authority, it provides a forum for developing, monitoring and reviewing the local child protection policies, and promoting effective and harmonious co-operation between the various agencies involved. Although there is some variation from area to area, each committee is made up of representatives of the key agencies, who have authority to speak and act on their agency's behalf. ACPCs issue guidelines about procedures, tackle significant issues that arise, offer advice about the conduct of cases in general, make policy and review progress on prevention, and oversee inter-agency training.

Assessment: A complex and skilled process of gathering together and evaluating information about a child, his/her family, and their circumstances. Its purpose is to determine children's needs, in order to plan for their immediate and long-term care, and decide what services and resources must be provided. Child care assessments are usually co-ordinated by Social Services, but depend upon teamwork with other agencies (such as education and health). Detailed information about conducting assessments in child protection cases is provided in *Protecting Children: a guide for social workers undertaking a comprehensive assessment* (Department of Health 1987).

Authorised person: In relation to care and supervision proceedings, a person other than the Local Authority, authorised by the Secretary of State to bring proceedings under Section 31 of the Act. This covers the NSPCC and its officers. Elsewhere in the Act there is a reference to persons who are authorised to carry out specified functions, eg to enter and inspect independent schools. You should refer to the relevant sections of the Act and the Regulations for further information on the powers of such authorised persons.

Care order: An order made by the court under Section 31(1)(a) of the Act placing the child in the care of the designated Local Authority. A care order includes an interim care order except where express provision to the contrary is made. [s31(11)]

Case conference: In a child care context, a formal meeting attended by representatives from all the agencies concerned with the child's welfare. Increasingly this includes the child's parents (and the Act promoted this practice). Its purpose is to gather together and evaluate all the relevant information about a child, and plan any immediate action which may be necessary to protect the child (eg seeking a court order). Where the meeting decides that the child and family need support, a key-worker will be appointed to co-ordinate an inter-agency plan for work with a child and the family, and the child's name (plus those of any other children living in the same household) may be entered on the Child Protection Register.

Child: A person under the age of eighteen. There is an important exception to this in the case of an application for financial relief by a 'child' who has reached eighteen and is, or will be, receiving education or training. [Sched 1, paras 2, 6 and 16]

Child assessment order: An order under Section 43 of the Act. The order requires any person who can do so to produce the child for an assessment and to comply with the terms of the order.

Child Protection Register: A central record of all children in a given area for whom support is being provided via inter-agency planning. Generally, these are children considered to be at risk of abuse or neglect. The register is usually maintained and run by Social Service Departments under the responsibility of a custodian (an experienced social worker able to provide advice to any professional making enquiries about the child). Registration for each child is reviewed every six months.

Child minder: A person who looks after one or more children under the age of eight for reward for more than two hours in any one day. [s71]

Children in need: A child is in need if (a) he is unlikely to achieve or maintain, or have the opportunity of achieving or maintaining, a reasonable standard of health or development without the provision for him of services by a Local Authority; (b) his health or development is likely to be significantly impaired, or further impaired, without the provision for him of such services; or (c) he is disabled. [s17(10)]

Children living away from home: Children who are not being looked after by the Local Authority but who are nevertheless living away from home – eg children in independent schools. The Local Authority has a number of duties towards such children, one of which is to take reasonably practicable steps to ensure that their welfare is being adequately safeguarded and promoted.

Complaints procedure: The procedure that the Local Authority must set up to hear representations regarding the provision of services under Part III of the Act from a number of persons, including the child, the parents and 'such other person as the authority considers has sufficient interest in the child's welfare to warrant his representations being considered by them'. [s26(3)] This procedure must contain an independent element.

Concurrent jurisdiction: By virtue of Section 92(7) the High Court, a county court and a magistrates' court (Family Proceedings Court) will have jurisdiction to hear all proceedings under the Act, with some clearly limited exceptions. It is also possible for all proceedings involving the same child and family, irrespective of where they started, to be heard in the same court.

Contact: Between a child and another person this includes visits, stays, outings and communication by letter and telephone. Under Section 34 of the Act, the Local Authority has a duty to allow a child in care reasonable contact with a number of persons, including the child's parents.

Contact order: An order 'requiring the person with whom a child lives, or is to live, to allow the child to visit or stay with the person named in the order, or for that person and the child otherwise to have contact with each other'. [s8]

Court welfare officer: An officer appointed to provide a report for the court about the child and the child's family situation and background. The court welfare officer will usually be a probation officer. The court may request either the Local Authority or the court welfare officer to prepare a report. [s7(1)]

Day care: A person provides day care if she/he looks after one or more children under the age of eight on non-domestic premises for more than two hours in any day. [s71] In relation to the Local Authority provision of day care, it refers to any form of supervised activity provided for children during the day. [s18(4)]

Development: Physical, intellectual, emotional, social or behavioural development. [s31(9)]

Disabled: A child is disabled if 'he is blind, deaf, or dumb or suffers from mental disorder of any kind or is substantially and permanently handicapped by illness, injury or congenital deformity or such other disability as may be prescribed'. [s17(11)]

Disclosure interview: A term sometimes used to describe an interview with a child conducted as part of the assessment for suspected sexual abuse. It is misleading since it implies, in some people's view, undue pressure on the child to 'disclose' so therefore the preferred term is 'investigative interview'.

Duty to investigate: The Local Authority has a duty to investigate in a number of situations. The general investigative duty arises where the Local Authority has a 'reasonable cause to suspect that a child who lives, or is found, in [its] area is suffering, or is likely to suffer, significant harm'. It must make such enquiries as it considers necessary to enable it to decide whether it should take any action to safeguard or promote the child's welfare. [s47(1)]

Educational psychologist: A psychology graduate who has had teaching experience and additional vocational training. Educational psychologists perform a range of functions, including assessing children's education, psychological and emotional needs, offering therapy and contributing psychological expertise to the process of assessment.

Education supervision order: An order under Section 36(1) which puts the child under the supervision of a designated Local Education Authority.

Education Welfare Officer (EWO): An EWO provides social work support to children in the context of their schooling. While EWOs' main focus used to be the enforcement of school attendance, today they perform a wider range of services, including seeking to ensure that children receive adequate and appropriate education and that any special needs are met, and more general liaison between Local Education Authorities and Social Services Departments. Their approach is primarily supportive and directed towards children's education entitlements.

Emergency protection order: An order under Section 44 which the court can make if it is satisfied that a child is likely to suffer significant harm, or where enquiries are being made with respect to the child and they are being frustrated by the unreasonable refusal of access to the child. The effect of the order is to operate as a direction to any persons in a position to do so to comply with any request to produce the child, and it authorises the removal of the child or the prevention of the child's removal. The order gives the applicant parental responsibility for the child. [s44]

Evidence: Section 96 of the Act allows a child who does not, in the opinion of the court, understand the nature of an oath, to give evidence if the court considers that the child understands that it is his/her duty to speak the truth and that she/he has sufficient understanding to justify the evidence being heard. Sections 7 and 41 permit the inclusion of what would be hearsay evidence (ie evidence of a fact not directly seen or heard by the witness) in reports written by social workers, court welfare officers and GALs.

Family assistance order: An order under Section 16 of the Act requiring either a probation officer or a social worker to 'advise, assist and befriend' a named person for a period of six months or less. The named person can be the child's parents, guardian, those with whom the child lived or who had contact with the child, and the child him/herself.

Family centre: A centre which the child and parents, and any other person looking after the child, can attend for occupational and recreational activities, advice, guidance or counselling, and accommodation while receiving such advice, guidance or counselling. [Sched 2 para 9]

Family panel: The new panel from which the magistrates who sit in the new family proceedings court are selected. These magistrates will have undergone specialist training on the Act.

Family proceedings: These are defined in Section 8(3) as any proceedings under the inherent jurisdiction of the High Court in relation to children; and under parts I, II and IV of the Act, the Matrimonial Causes Act 1973, the Domestic Violence and Matrimonial Proceedings Act 1976, the Adoption Act 1976, the Domestic Proceedings and Magistrates' Courts Act 1978, Sections 1 and 9 of the Matrimonial Homes Act 1983, and Part III of the Matrimonial and Family Proceedings Act 1984. Note: proceedings under Part V of the Children Act 1989, ie orders for the protection of children, are not family proceedings.

Family proceedings court: The new court at the level of the magistrates' court to hear proceedings under the Children Act 1989. The magistrates will be selected from a new panel, known as the family panel, and will be specially trained.

Fieldworker (field social worker): Conducts a range of social work functions in the community and in other settings (eg hospitals). Most fieldworkers carry their own case load, and, following career progression, undertake supervision of others and/or specialise either with a particular group (eg older people) or in a particular function (eg running the home-help service). In many (but by no means all) Local Authorities, specialist social workers have been appointed to co-ordinate child protection work and offer particular expertise, for example in conducting joint investigative interviews with police officers.

Foster-carer: A foster-carer provides substitute family care for children. A child looked after by a Local Authority can be placed with Local Authority foster-carers under Section 23(2)(a). Under the Act, Part IX regulates the private foster-care of children for more than twenty-seven days. Private foster-carers are subject to the usual fostering limit of three children unless they are siblings or the Local Authority grants them an exemption. Short-term care of children under eight may be subject to the child-minding provisions in Part X.

Guardian *ad litem* (GAL): A person appointed by the court to investigate a child's circumstances and to report to the court. The GAL does not represent the child but seeks to present a non-partisan view of the child's welfare.

The GAL can appoint a solicitor for the child. In some cases the official solicitor acts as the GAL.

Guidance: Local Authorities are required to act in accordance with the guidance issued by the Secretary of State. However, guidance does not have the full force of law but is intended as a series of statements of good practice and may be quoted or used in court proceedings.

Harm: Defined as 'ill-treatment or the impairment of health or development'. [s31(9)]

Health: Physical or mental health.

Ill-treatment: This includes sexual abuse and forms of ill-treatment which are not physical.

In care: This refers to a child in the care of the Local Authority by virtue of an order under Section 31(1)(a) or an interim order under Section 38 of the Act.

Independent visitor: The Local Authority in certain circumstances appoints such a visitor for a child it is looking after. The visitor appointed has a duty of 'visiting, advising and befriending the child'. [Sched 2, para 7)

Inherent jurisdiction: The powers of the High Court to make orders to protect a child, which are not based on statute and which are outside the established wardship jurisdiction.

Injunction: An order made by the court prohibiting an act or requiring its cessation. Under the Domestic Violence and Matrimonial Proceedings Act 1976 the county court has the power to make injunctions. Injunctions can be either interlocutory (ie temporary, pending the outcome of the full hearing) or perpetual.

Inter-agency plan: A plan devised jointly by the agencies concerned in a child's welfare which co-ordinates the services they provide. Its aim is to ensure that the support offered meets all the child's needs, so far as this is practicable, and that duplication and rivalry are avoided. The plan should specify goals to be achieved, resources and services to be provided, the allocation of responsibilities, and arrangements for monitoring and review.

Interim care order: An order made by the court under Section 38 placing the child in the care of the designated Local Authority. There are complex provisions as to its duration, with a special initial period of eight weeks. There is no limit to the number of interim care orders that can be made.

Interim supervision order: See **Interim care order**.

Investigative interview: The preferred term for an interview conducted with a child as part of an assessment following concerns that the child may have been abused (most notably, in cases of suspected sexual abuse). In many areas these interviews are conducted jointly by specially trained social workers and police officers, in order to reduce the number of times children are expected to tell their story and for information to be gathered in ways that make it acceptable as evidence, if the need arises.

Judicial review: An order from the divisional court quashing a disputed decision. The divisional court cannot substitute its own decision, but can merely send the matter back to the offending authority for reconsideration.

Keyworker: A social worker allocated specific responsibility for a particular child. In residential settings, this person will maintain an overall interest in the child's welfare, and they will often undertake specific work with the child on a day-to-day basis. In a fieldwork child-care setting, the keyworker is appointed at a case conference, and is responsible for co-ordinating the work done with and for the child by the different agencies (eg health, education, housing).

Legal aid: This is available in proceedings under the Act. There is neither a merits nor means test in relation to proceedings under Section 25 relating to secure accommodation.

Looked after: A child is looked after when she/he is in Local Authority care or is being provided with accommodation by the Local Authority. [s22(1)]

Monitoring: Where plans for a child and the child's safety and well-being are systematically appraised on a routine basis. Its function is to oversee the child's continued welfare and enable any necessary action or change to be instigated speedily, and, at a managerial level, to ensure that proper professional standards are being maintained.

Official solicitor: An officer of the Supreme Court who acts on behalf of children in certain cases. When representing, the official solicitor acts as a solicitor as well as a guardian *ad litem*.

Paramountcy principle: The principle that the welfare of the child is of paramount consideration in proceedings concerning children.

Parental responsibility: Defined as 'all the rights, duties, powers, responsibilities and authority which by law a parent of a child has in relation to the child and his property'. [s3(1)] Parental responsibility can be exercised by persons who are not the child's biological parents and can be shared among a number of persons. It can be acquired by agreement or court order.

Parties: Parties to proceedings are entitled to attend the hearing, present their case and examine witnesses. The Act envisages that children will automatically be parties in case proceedings. Anyone with parental responsibility for the child will also be a party to such proceedings, as will the Local Authority. Others may be able to acquire party status. A person with party status will be eligible for legal aid in order to be legally represented at the hearing. If you have party status you are also able to appeal against the decision. Others who are not parties may be entitled to make representations. For further information on this, refer to the Rules of Court.

Permanency planning: Deciding on the long-term future of children who have been moved from their families. Its purpose is to ensure them a permanent, stable and secure upbringing, either within their original family or by providing high-quality alternative parenting (for example, living permanently with grandparents or other relatives, or being adopted). Its aim is to avoid long periods of insecurity or repeated disruptions in children's lives. Hence it should be completed speedily, preferably within six months of a child first moving away from home.

Police protection: Section 46 allows the police to detain a child or prevent his/her removal for up to seventy-two hours if they believe that the child would otherwise suffer significant harm. There are clear duties on the police to consult the child, if this is practicable, and to notify various persons of their action, eg the child's parents and the Local Authority.

Preliminary hearing: A hearing to clarify matters in dispute, to agree evidence, and to give directions as to the timetable of the case and the disclosure of evidence.

Probation officer: A welfare professional employed as an officer of the court and financed jointly by the Local Authority and the Home Office. In addition to taking on a case-load, most probation officers undertake some specialist work, such as conducting group work with offenders or helping to run a phone-in service. An important role is the provision of welfare reports of various kinds.

Prohibited steps order: An order that 'no step which could be taken by a parent in meeting his parental responsibility for a child, and which is of a kind specified in the order, shall be taken by any person without the consent of the court'. [s8(1)]

Recovery order: An order which the court can make when there is reason to believe that a child who is in care, the subject of an emergency protection order or in police protection, has been unlawfully taken or kept away from the responsible person, or is missing. The effect of the recovery order is to require any person who is in a position to do so, to produce the child on request, to authorise the removal of the child by any authorised person, and to require any person who has information as to the child's whereabouts, to disclose that information if asked to do so, to a constable or officer of the court. [s50]

Refuge: Section 51 enables 'safe houses' legally to provide care for children who have run away from home or Local Authority care. However, a recovery order can be obtained in relation to a child who has run away to a refuge.

Regulations: Refer to the supplementary powers and duties issued by the Secretary of State under the authority of the Act. These cover a wide range of issues, from secure accommodation to the procedure for considering representations (including complaints), and have the full force of law.

Rehabilitation: In a child-care context, the process of working with children and parents, and providing resources and support to enable children to return home and be brought up by their families, for the children's needs to be met, and to help overcome the problems that led to their needing to live away.

Representations: See **Complaints procedure.**

Residence order: An order 'settling the arrangements to be made as to the person with whom a child is to live'. [s8(1)]

Residential social worker: He or she provides day-to-day care, support and therapy for children living in residential settings, such as children's homes. Until recently most residential social workers were unqualified. As the importance and demands of their work have become increasingly recognised, more training opportunities are being provided.

Respite care: A service giving family members or other carers short breaks from their caring responsibilities. It is intended to support the care of people (eg those with disabilities or infirmities) in the community who might otherwise need to be placed in full-time residential care.

Responsible person: In relation to a supervised child, 'any person who has parental responsibility for the child, and any other person with whom the child is living'. With their consent, the responsible person can be required to comply with certain obligations. [Sched 3, paras 1 and 3]

Review: Under Section 26 Local Authorities have a duty to conduct regular reviews in order to monitor the progress of children they are looking after. When holding reviews, Local Authorities must comply with their duties as given in Section 22. Reviews are opportunities to consider progress and any problems and changes in circumstances, and to resolve difficulties, set new goals and plan for the future. They are usually attended by all those with significant responsibilities for the child. The child and his/her parents should also attend, and be given help and support to participate in the decision-making and to make sure their views and wishes are known. [s26]

Rules: Rules of Court produced by the Lord Chancellor's Department and the Home Office. These lay down the procedural rules which govern the operation of the courts under the Children Act 1989.

Section 8 orders: The four new orders contained in the Act which, to varying degrees, regulate the exercise of parental responsibility.

Secure accommodation: Section 25 provides for the circumstances in which a child who is being looked after by the Local Authority can be placed in secure accommodation. Such accommodation is provided for the purpose of restricting the liberty of the child.

Significant harm: Section 31(10) states: 'Where the question of whether harm suffered by the child is significant turns on the child's health or development, his health or development shall be compared with that which could reasonably be expected of a similar child.'

Social worker: A generic term applying to a wide range of staff who undertake different kinds of social welfare responsibilities. These include advising and supporting individuals and families during periods of trouble, both within the community and in residential settings; conducting assessments and investigations and monitoring standards of care. Social workers may be employed by Local Authorities, courts or voluntary organisations (see **Residential social worker**; **Fieldworker**; **Education Welfare Officer** and **Probation officer**).

Specific issue order: An order 'giving directions for the purpose of determining a specific question which has arisen, or which may arise, in connection with any aspect of parental responsibility for a child'. [s8(1)]

Supervision order: An order under Section 31(1)(b) and including, except where express contrary provision is made, an interim supervision order under Section 38. [s31]

Supervisor: The person under whose supervision the child is placed by virtue of an order under Sections 31 and 38. The powers and duties of the supervisor are contained in Section 35 and Schedule 3.

Timetables: Under the Act, the court, pursuant to the principle of avoiding delay because it is harmful for the child, has the power to draw up a timetable and give directions for the conduct of the case in any proceedings in which the making of a Section 8 order arises, and in applications for care and supervision orders. [ss11 and 32]

Transitional arrangements: The arrangements relating to children who are the subjects of existing orders under legislation prior to the implementation of the Children Act 1989. The general rule is that where this is the case, the child will be treated as if she/he were the subject of the nearest equivalent order in the Act.

Ward of court: A child who, as the subject of wardship proceedings, is under the protection of the High Court. No important decision can be taken regarding the child while she/he is a ward of court without the consent of the wardship court.

Wardship: The legal process whereby control is exercised over the child in order to protect the child and safeguard his/her welfare.

Welfare checklist: This refers to the inventory checklist contained in Section 1(3) of the Act. This checklist applies in all contested Section 8 proceedings and all proceedings under Part IV of the Act. It does not apply in proceedings under Part V of the Act on child protection.

Welfare report: Section 7 of the Act gives the court the power to request a report on any question in respect of a child under the Act. The report can be presented by either a probation officer or an officer of the Local Authority. Section 7(4) provides that regardless of any rule of law to the contrary, the court may take account of any statement contained in the report and any evidence given in respect of matters referred to in the report as long as the court considers them relevant.

Written agreement: The agreement arrived at between the Local Authority and the parents of children for whom it is providing services. These arrangements are part of the partnership model that is seen as good practice under the Act.

(Taken from *The Children Act 1989: An Introductory Guide for the NHS* (HMSO).

9

Feasibility Studies and Consultancy

I have mentioned in previous chapters the importance of feasibility studies and adequate research prior to setting up a project, but I feel that the subject warrants some more specific treatment. Most people approach a project with great enthusiasm, willing hearts and able bodies. They also spend a considerable amount of time fund-raising, waiting on God and praying for wisdom. But on occasions the obvious can be missed. The enthusiasm of the team, individual or group seeking to set up a project can result in people acting in response to a need without first ascertaining what needs are already being met by existing services within the community. Christian organisations tend also to work in isolation, not discussing their proposed plans with other organisations. This may result in several similar projects being set up in the same geographical area. More confusion can be caused when these groups are all in separate discussions with fundholders in local government. A feasibility study can help resolve many of these issues.

I would recommend that an independent specialist is appointed to carry out the study, although this work could be done by someone within the planning group. An outside approach would be more objective, and more time would be devoted to carrying out the research. This would obviously cost a great deal more than using someone in the planning group but should supply appropriate and accurate information about issues a layman may not consider. The needs of the local area and information on existing projects are primary to the study. Discussions with statutory bodies and voluntary agencies about the type of project planned and whether or not they would be sympathetic to the work or able to support it in any way also need to take place. I have found on many occasions through my work on such studies for projects for the homeless, children's holiday centres, single-parent day and residential units and counselling centres, that as an outside consultant I am given help and information not normally available to groups whose work is not clearly defined.

A completed study can also be used for fund-raising purposes, as part of an information pack to statutory and voluntary agencies, as ongoing data on the way the project could proceed, and as part of a business plan for banks or other financial institutions including grant-awarding charities. The awarding bodies tend to see those organisations which commission a feasibility study as being more professional and realistic in their approach to the work they are planning. Once a feasibility study has been completed it is recommended that the same organisation or consultant be used as an advisor by the management group or the project organisers. This may seem rather grand, but in practice it is very simple and could help support the project through the 'teething' problems of the early stages. I would strongly recommend this to those involved in para-church organisations, the new church movement and those churches and individuals who do not have back-up within their organisations to supply consultancy support.

When choosing an individual to complete a feasibility study it is important that they have wide knowledge in the sphere of your planned project. If the project is to be in the community working with the homeless, children, adults with learning difficulties, those with mental health problems, citizens' advice or counselling, the person chosen to complete the study should be familiar with the workings of Social Services, Health Trusts, voluntary agencies, the Community Care Act and the Children Act, as well as legislation in counselling and concepts of training. Organisations very often call upon the expertise of a psychologist, psychiatrist, doctor, counsellor, lawyer, pastor or therapist. These are all capable within their own field, but they may not be the most suitable people to implement a feasibility study.

A feasibility study should include the following (not listed in order of priority):

- A complete history of the organisation/church to present day
- The value base of the organisation/church
- The aims and objectives of the feasibility study
- Type of project proposed
- Research into the subject of the project

- A national and local overview of provision in this area from all sectors
- Current legislation pertinent to project
- Local population
- In-depth study of target group
- Availability of other resources

- Finance
- Possible funding/grants

- Ideal type of property needed
- Availability of property and cost
- Planning permission and building regulations
- Management structure

- Staffing
- Team-building

- Training
- Literature

A separate financial plan should be completed by an accountant to complement the feasibility study. This financial plan in conjunction with the feasibility study should help establish whether or not the proposed project is viable. Having invested time and effort into the study, it is most important that the planning group agree to take heed of its findings and final report. God does sometimes call us to work against what seems possible in the natural realm, but if everything else points towards imminent disaster maybe it would be wise to wait on God again for confirmation.

Any project, whatever the area of work, will need consultancy advice at some point and contingency plans can be made for this eventuality. A council of reference is one way of having sympathetic expertise available. The precise make-up of such a council would obviously vary according to the project, but alongside the accountant and lawyer (who have already been pointed out as essential components of any project), individuals with specific skill in relevant areas, such as psychiatrist, psychologist, GP, individuals with particular ministry gifts (prayer, healing, deliverance, etc), specialist counsellors, trainers and those involved in similar projects could also be considered. Many may be willing and able to give regular time to the project, while others will just be available for a particular need. There may be need for financial response for advice given, and this should be established from the outset. It is essential that any consultant is sympathetic to the value base from which the project works and understands the aims and objectives. Keeping the consultants up to date with the ongoing work through newsletters or other literature would help to promote good relationships and a sense of team.

10

Summary

Over the last five years we have seen a process of continual change within health care, Social Services and education. Alongside this there have also been major changes taking place in the church setting. These modifications will continue well into the next century and the church will need to be equipped to deal with them as it works in the community, particularly when establishing new projects. We are already being made aware of a major challenge to Christian organisations in the United States which have set up rehabilitation centres and community projects. There is a possibility that funding for these projects will be withdrawn due to the lack of qualifications held by those working at the centres offering Christian ministry and therapy. Although these projects have been successful, it is being questioned as to whether or not they should continue without qualified professional staff. We are beginning to see a similar situation arise in the UK and other parts of Europe, where Christian organisations are seeking government, Local Authority or European funding. There could well be a request that all staff, especially managers, carers and counsellors, are accredited, qualified or on a UK register. This marks a major change for the church and particularly for volunteers, although it will probably be some time before it affects the church, as the government will look at professional agencies first.

It is essential that we seek to offer the highest standards

of good practice to those we care for. There is need for prayer, careful planning, research, training and good management to enable and equip us to prevent those who are already hurting from being further damaged by bad practice, closure of projects or inappropriate procedures. Supervision and support are key elements for all those working within the caring and counselling arena. Working along with God-given commonsense should provide a formula for success.

For all who set out on a journey which includes working with other people setting up projects, it is an exciting journey – especially when we see that God can rebuild people's lives where others have declared it impossible.

Appendices

APPENDIX A

Setting up a Counselling Agency in the Pastoral/Church Setting (Personnel)

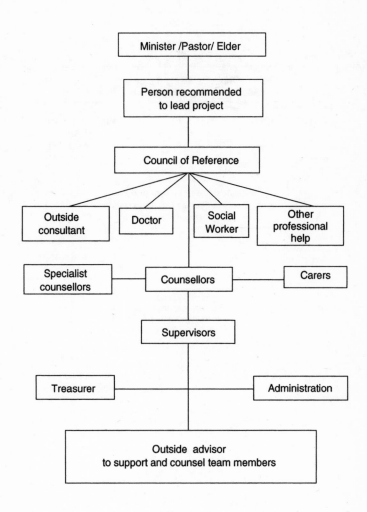

Setting up a Christian Counselling Team (Components)

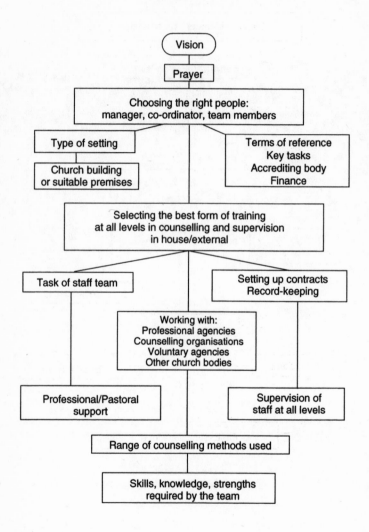

APPENDIX B

Suggested Team Structure

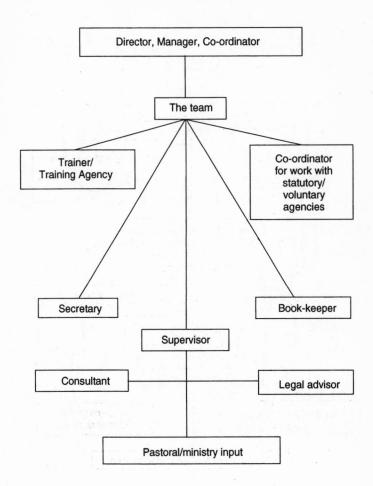

APPENDIX C

COUNSELLING ENVIRONMENT

Comfort
- Type of Seating
- Tissues
- Refreshments?
- Toilets
- Seating Position
  - Lighting and Glare
  - Distractions
  - Distractions
- Pets
  - Allergies
  - Fears

Counselling Room
- Decor
- Accessibility
- Odours
- Tidiness
- Cleanliness

Distractions
- Internal Noise
- Children
- External Noise
- Other counsellors
- Other Clients
- Telephones
- Pets

Counsellor
- Appropriate Dress
- No Distractions
- Grooming
- Unhurried
- Well Prepared
- Breath
- Personal Hygiene
- Body Odour

APPENDIX D

The Counselling Contract
Confidential

Date of initial interview .... Carried out by ....

Age: Under 18 (specify) ...... 18–29 ...... 30–49 ......
50–59 ...... 60 or over ......

Marital status ....
Relevant family details ....
....
....

How did the client hear about us? ....

Is he/she seeing anyone else? Please tick:
Psychiatrist Psychologist Social Worker Solicitor Counsellor Minister

Doctor – If yes, GP's name and address ....
....
....

Details of medication if any ....
....

Details of any recent medical problems, previous major illness or
nervous disorder ....
....
....
....

Does he/she attend church NO/YES
Where ....
Minister's/church leader's name ....
Does the minister/church leader know we are being contacted? NO/YES
Is there any objection to the minister/church leader knowing? NO/YES
Any dates or times when he/she is unavailable for counselling? ....
....

Working agreement between Barnabas House and ...... (Name of client)

The purpose

The reason for this agreement is to ensure that there is a clear understanding of the basis upon which Barnabas House will be working with a client.

What is Barnabas House?

Barnabas House is a registered charity based in Carmarthen. It is run by committed Christians who are seeking to serve and support those who are in need.

Code of conduct

Our code of conduct clearly emphasises the rights, choices and respect for individuals. As Christians we believe that everyone is unique and of equal value; we seek to serve others in a non-judgemental, non-superior way.

Confidentiality

Confidentiality is a key element in our practice, but due consideration should be given before disclosing anything of a criminal nature to a counsellor as Barnabas House may have a legal obligation to report such matter.

Exceptional circumstances may arise which give the Director good grounds for believing that the client will cause serious physical harm to others or to himself/herself or may have harm caused to him/her. Whenever possible in such circumstances the client's permission will be sought before breaking confidentiality.

We have a moral and at times legal obligation to inform social services of any recent or current acts of sexual or physical abuse upon a child and will inform the client accordingly.

We operate as a team and are all under supervision.

Confidentiality will always be kept within the team subject to the comments made above.

If appropriate, Barnabas House may seek permission to contact other agencies, members of the medical profession or minister/church leader. Subsequently if it is in the client's best interest a referral to one of these parties may be suggested.

As standard professional procedure summary notes of all meetings with the client will be taken. These will be coded to maintain confidentiality and will be kept in a locked cupboard.

Availability

An initial appraisal meeting will be arranged according to availability of a team member.

Future meetings will be by appointment – the client is asked to inform the centre if unable to keep an appointment.

Meetings will normally be for one hour, so punctuality is important. The frequency of appointments will be arranged in agreement with the counsellor.

Meetings will be with one or two members of the Barnabas House team. If it is thought to be in the client's best interest, or in the case of illness, another member of the team may be introduced into meetings.

Existing help

If the client is on medication he/she should remain on it.

If the client is under a professional agency or if he/she is seeing a doctor, psychiatrist, or any other professional he/she should continue.

Complaints procedure

If for any reason the client is unhappy with any aspect of his/her involvement with Barnabas House this should

initially be discussed with the counsellor, and if a satisfactory solution cannot be found comments should be put
in writing and addressed to the Centre Director.

Third party discussion will not be entered into.

Payments

Barnabas House provides its services free of charge as part
of its service to the community but donations are always
very acceptable.

Client's responsibility

The client is free to leave counselling at any stage, though
he/she may be advised to consult his/her doctor or another
counsellor.

The client will remain responsible at all times for his/
her actions. Barnabas House does not accept liability for
personal injury, death or loss of belongings.

Barnabas House retains the right to terminate this contract
at its discretion.

The client's statutory rights are in no way affected by
any of the terms in this agreement.

I have read the above and agree to abide by the conditions
set out.

Signed ....
                          Client   for Barnabas House

Date ....   Date ....

Confidential counselling appraisal form

Nature of problem stated:

Key points from appraisal:

Future action:
How urgent is it?

Referral elsewhere

Appointment made for Barnabas House

COUNSELLING DIARY

Date	Counsellor(s)	General notes	Key points/ homework

All counsellors are required to agree to the following:

1. To work under supervision
2. To work under the guidelines given by the trustees
3. To abide by the code of ethics (ACC, BAC, other)
4. To be a paid-up member of a professional body
5. To be aware of the complaints procedure
6. To take part in ongoing training – in house and external
7. To abide by a written contract.

Any referrals to Barnabas House need to be made in writing and agreed by the directors of the Trust. The first counselling session will be an assessment only and if a contract is drawn up between client, counsellor and agency it will be for an initial six weeks and a review.

Referral from:

Doctor ☐
Health Trust ☐
Social Services ☐
Probation ☐
Self ☐
Agency ☐
Church ☐
Counsellor ☐

Agreed Fee ☐
Letter sent ☐ Date ....

Agenda and dates agreed ☐ Date ....

Signed: Director of Barnabas House ....
Signed: Representative of Agency ....
          Designation ....

Example of a Counselling Contract for Outside Referrals

Contract between Barnabas House, Wales and ....

Barnabas House, Wales, is a Christian organisation working in a pastoral and community setting offering day counselling, residential care and counselling, work with families and a variety of stress-related issues. Barnabas House, Wales, adheres to the Association of Christian Counsellors' and British Association of Counsellors' code of ethics and operates an equal opportunities policy.

The initial agreement will be for six sessions on either a weekly or fortnightly basis and a review on the seventh session. This review will take place between the Director of Barnabas House, the counsellor and referring agency. This will be an important part of the ongoing work with the client and the point at which the decision to close down will be taken. If a trust or other agency wishes to use our agency, a longer contract with six- or twelve-weekly reviews can be established.

6 weeks	☐
12	☐
18	☐
24	☐
30	☐

Barnabas House is a registered charity (700902) and does not always charge a fee for its counselling services, except in regard to residential accommodation, where a possible agreed fee will be negotiated with the referring agency. Please tick preferred method of payment:

sessionally ☐
monthly ☐
quarterly ☐
six monthly ☐
annually ☐
no fee ☐

Barnabas House is funded by organisations throughout the UK and individual gifts. The organisation is accountable to a board of trustees and has a council of reference for specialist advice and support. All counsellors are accredited or working towards accreditation and the organisation operates a complaints procedure. If a complaint is made by a client it will initially be dealt with by the counsellor involved and if a satisfactory resolution is not found it will be referred first to the manager and then to the trustees. If the complaint is still not resolved the client will be at liberty to take the complaint on to BAC or ACC, as Barnabas House is a member of both organisations.

Barnabas House has professional indemnity cover along with third party liability. To enhance the work of Barnabas House a group of professionals including solicitors, doctors, therapists and specialist counsellors are available when their services are required.

APPENDIX E

Possible Issues Arising in Counselling

Interpersonal relationships
a) Communication skills
b) Conflict resolution
c) Family relationships
d) Work relationships
e) Relationships in society

Children and parents
a) Problems with parenting
b) Babies
c) Bringing up young children
d) Adolescence
e) Child abuse
f) Adoption:
   (i) Adopted children
   (ii) Parents with adopted children
   (iii) Mothers who have children adopted
   (iv) Surrogacy
   (v) Fostering
g) School
h) Single parents
i) Step-parents

Self-esteem
a) Self-awareness
b) Poor self-esteem
c) Loneliness
d) Anger
e) Guilt
f) Bitterness and unforgiveness
g) Body-image problems

Marital problems
a) Pre-marital counselling
b) Sex in marriage
c) Problems with pregnancy
d) Infertility/surrogacy
e) Family planning
f) Marital relationship problems
g) Separation and divorce
h) Re-marriage
i) Extra-marital sexual relationships
j) Widows and widowers

The family
a) Nuclear family dynamics
b) Dysfunctional family dynamics
c) Cultural differences
d) Family types
e) Problems in families
f) The family in crisis

Trauma
a) Natural disasters
b) Accidents
c) Murder and manslaughter

Stress
a) Definitions of stress
b) Normal and abnormal stress
c) Burn-out
d) Caring for carers

Acute illness
a) Associated mental and emotional problems
b) Practical help
c) Convalescence

Health education and lifestyle
a) Physical fitness
b) Health
c) Special diets (eg vegan)
d) Exercise
e) Changing habits

Addictions
a) Gambling
b) Drug addiction
c) Alcohol
d) Smoking
e) Substance abuse

Bereavement and grief
a) Normal process of grieving
b) Bereavement process
c) Abnormal grief reactions
d) Caring for the dying
e) Facing death
f) Death of children
g) Dying at home
h) Miscarriage

Race and culture
a) Mixed culture marriages
b) Cross-cultural counselling
c) Adjusting to new culture

Chronic illness
a) Arthritis and other mobility problems
b) Associated mental problems
c) Allergies
d) AIDS
e) Keeping healthy

Mental problems
a) Anxiety neuroses
b) Psychoses and psychopathic behaviour
c) Affective disorder
d) Obsessive neuroses
e) Eating disorders:
   (i)   Anorexia nervosa
   (ii) Bulimia
   (iii) Obesity

Age-related problems
a) Middle-age in men
b) Middle-age in women:
   (i) Menopause
   (ii) 'Empty nest' syndrome
c) Senility
d) Caring for the elderly
e) Sex and the elderly
f) Elderly parents

Unwanted pregnancy
a) Within marriage
b) Illegitimate pregnancy
c) Pre-abortion
d) Post-abortion
e) Adoption

Sexuality

a) Sexual development
b) Homosexuality
c) Sexual perversions
d) Prostitution
e) Rape
f) Sexual abuse
g) Masturbation
h) Sex outside marriage
i) Sexual problems in the female:
   (i) Frigidity
   (ii) Vaginismus
j) Sexual problems in the male:
   (i) Impotence
   (ii) Premature ejaculation
k) Sexual matters and the physically/sensory handicapped and those with learning difficulties
l) Sexual identity
m) Contraception
n) Pornography
o) Sexually transmitted diseases

Singleness

a) Crisis periods
   (i)   25–30
   (ii) 35–40
   (iii) 45–50
   (iv) 55–60 (retirement)
b) Loneliness
c) Family expectations
d) Fulfilment
e) Identity
f) Place in the Christian community

g) Loss
h) Sexuality

Religious beliefs

a) Various religious beliefs
b) Religious cults
c) Ex-cult members
d) Families of people involved in cults
e) Satanism and the occult

Work-related problems

a) The workaholic
b) Stress at work
c) Employee/employer relationships
d) Redundancy
e) Unemployment
f) Retirement

Finances

a) Budgeting
b) Debt
c) Financial problems

Social Services and the Welfare State

a) Social Services
b) DSS
c) Health services
d) Probation Service
e) Prison Service
f) Legal services
g) Citizens' Advice Bureau
h) Children Act
i) Community Care Act

Counselling in the Community Setting

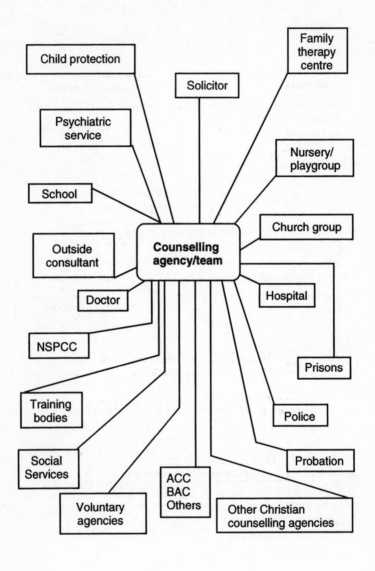

APPENDIX G

Setting up a Counselling Agency

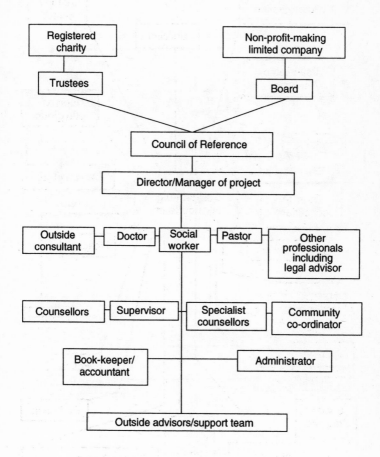

```
Registered                              Non-profit-making
charity                                 limited company

    Trustees                                    Board

                    Council of Reference

                    Director/Manager of project

Outside      Doctor    Social    Pastor    Other
consultant             worker               professionals
                                            including
                                            legal advisor

Counsellors   Supervisor    Specialist     Community
                            counsellors     co-ordinator

    Book-keeper/                    Administrator
    accountant

            Outside advisors/support team
```

Setting up a Day Care/Residential Project in the Pastoral or Community Setting

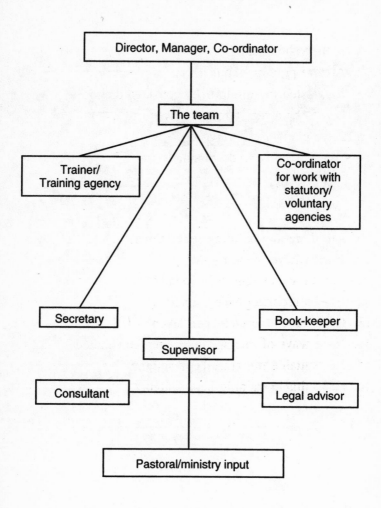

APPENDIX H(i)

Checklist for Church-Based Projects, Registered Charities, and Non-Profit-Making Limited Companies

1. Is the vision clear?
2. Are we praying about it?
3. Has a steering group been considered/chosen?
4. Is it to be a registered charity/trust?
5. Have plans been drawn up?
6. Is a feasibility study planned?
7. Has planning permission been sought?
8. Has planning permission for change of use been sought?
9. Are there any building regulations?
10. Has a lawyer been found?
11. Has an accountant been found?
12. Has an architect been found?
13. Has financial advice been taken?
14. Have ways of raising funds been considered?
15. Has suitable literature been sought?
16. Has suitable training been sought?

APPENDIX I

Supervision Agreement

Name of agency/organisation . . . .
Name of supervisee . . . .
Name of supervisor . . . .
Practical arrangements:

Frequency: Length:

Day: Time: Place:

Responsibilities:

Agenda   Notes   Preparation

The supervisor will be responsible for:

The supervisee will be responsible for:

Confidentiality:

The confidential nature of the supervision process will be maintained by:

Expectations/attitudes/comments/priorities

As Supervisor I expect . . . .
. . . .
As Supervisee I expect . . . .
. . . .
Any other terms that either may wish to include in the agreement.

Signed . . . . **Supervisor**
         . . . . **Supervisee**
Date: . . . .

APPENDIX I(i)

Checklist for Formal Supervision

Has an agenda been produced?

Have I carried out the decisions made at our last session?

Have I checked if my supervisee has items for inclusion?

Have I set aside time to prepare?

Have I booked a quiet room/place?

Are there staff to cover to avoid unnecessary interruptions?

Am I making the best use of arrangements, relationships and environment?

Do I enjoy these sessions? If not, why not?

What difficult areas might there be?

What encouragement can I give?

Is the agreement being maintained?

Does it need to change?

Should I involve anyone else?

Am I keeping a balance between managing/educating/ supporting?

Is my style of supervision appropriate?

Am I using all the skills?

Am I learning from these sessions?

Have I set a date for the next session?

Have I allocated time to evaluate?

Did the agenda/plan work?

What were the problems, if any?

Did I give my supervisee space to talk?

What did we both learn from the session?

What was good about the session?

What will improve next time?

Recommended Reading

Hurding, Roger. *Roots and Shoots*. Hodder & Stoughton: London, 1985.

An in-depth Christian study book on counselling models and processes. An essential reference book for the Christian counsellor. Very well written, but definitely not bedtime reading.

Hepden, Steve. *Rejection*. Sovereign World: Kent, 1992.

The subject of rejection is covered from childhood to adulthood. An excellent book for counsellors working in this area. It is also a useful small book to give to clients to read for themselves.

Johnson, David and Van Vonderon, Jeff. *The Subtle Power of Spiritual Abuse*. Bethany House: Minneapolis, USA, 1991.

An excellent Christian book which all pastors, leaders and others involved in Christian counselling should read. It is easy to read and understand, and deals with the misuse of power in the church setting.

Rutter, Peter. *Sex in the Forbidden Zone*. Mandela: Glasgow, 1989.

A secular book covering the misuse of power by professionals, doctors, therapists, church leaders and anyone in a position of authority. It deals particularly, but not exclusively, with areas where women's trust has been broken during therapy when boundaries have been crossed.

Dryden, Windy. *Brief Counselling*. Open University Press: 1992.

An excellent secular book for those starting out in counselling. It gives very clear guidelines on the process of counselling.

Heron, John. *Helping the Client.* Sage.

A secular book which covers the various processes and terms used in counselling. I would recommend this book to those already involved in counselling and helping people.

Matthews, Cathy Ann. *Breaking Through.* Albatross Books: Australia, 1990.

An autobiography of child abuse and working through the consequences. A Christian book suitable for counsellor and client.

Newman, Rebecca. *Releasing the Scream.* Hodder & Stoughton: London, 1994.

Another autobiographical account of child abuse and the journey to wholeness. Another Christian book suitable for both counsellor and client.

Pfiefer, Samuel. *Supporting the Weak.* Word Books: Milton Keynes, 1994.

An excellent Christian book dealing with the mind and hurting people. It is written by a psychiatrist in everyday language and is suitable for pastors, leaders and counsellors.

Allender, Dan. *Wounded Heart.* CWR: Farnham, 1990.

Another Christian book ideal for those working with or supporting the abused. A well-written book which covers all types of abuse, giving case studies and ways of helping. A useful reference book for the counsellor. Could also be used with the counsellee, but with caution. A work book is available.

Atkinson, Sue. *Climbing out of Depression.* Lion: Oxford, 1993.

An easy-to-read, practical book suitable for pastors, leaders and counsellors, as well as those working in the caring professions. It contains some helpful guidelines for coping with depression. Could be given to a counsellee for self-help.

Worden, William. *Grief Counselling and Grief Therapy.* Routledge: USA, 1983.

One of the best secular books on the subject. Helpful for those working with the bereaved and for the bereaved themselves.

Feltham, Colin and Dryden, Windy. *Developing Supervision.* Sage: London, 1994.

A good, all-round secular book for those starting out in supervision. Recommended by ACC for supervisors and counsellors.

Duffy, Wendy. *Children and Bereavement.* National Society/Church House Publishing: London, 1995.

A Christian book for those working with children who are going through the grieving process. A sensitive guide to the needs of children of different ages. Written in reader-friendly style.

Noonan, Ellen. *Counselling Young People.* Routledge: London, 1989.

A comprehensive guide for those dealing with young people in the community setting. Offers guidance on a wide range of skills, theory and practice.

Payne, Leanne. *The Broken Image.* Kingsway: Eastbourne, 1981.

An excellent Christian book for those supporting others who have experienced sexual brokenness. Sets clear guidelines and principles in simple language.

Harding, Linda. *Better Than or Equal To?* Word Books: Milton Keynes, 1993.

A Christian book which is an excellent guide for those dealing with the issues of singleness. A useful resource for the church and individuals. Raises awareness of the issues of singleness, our attitudes and responses.

APPENDIX K

Useful Resources

Association of Christian Counsellors (ACC)

175 Wokingham Road, Reading, Berkshire RG6 1LT (Tel 01734 662207).

British Association of Counselling (BAC)

1 Regent Street, Rugby, Warwickshire CV21 2PJ (Tel 01788 578328; Fax 01788 550899).

Barnabas Training Consortium/Barnabas House, Wales (BTC)

Salem Chapel, Salem Road, Johnstown, Carmarthen, Dyfed SA31 3HJ (Tel 01267 230428).

Christian Action in Research and Education (CARE)

53 Romney Street, London SW1P 3RF (Tel 0171 233 0455).

CARE for the Family

136 Newport Road, Roath, Cardiff CF2 1DJ (Tel 01222 494431).

PCCA Christian Child Care

PO Box 133, Swanley, Kent BR8 7UQ (Tel 01322 667207).

The Christian Counsellor's Directory

Obtainable from Christian Resource Centre, Salem Chapel, Salem Road, Johnstown, Carmarthen, Dyfed SA31 3HJ (Tel 01267 230428).

Local Child Protection Handbook

Obtainable from Social Services Department.

Registration of Homes Act 1984

Policy and Procedure Handbook obtainable from Social Services Department or Registration and Inspection Unit.

The Introductory Guide for NHS to the Children Act 1989

Obtainable from HMSO.

Working Together

HMSO.

A series of guides for children and young people and parents on the Children Act 1989:

The Children Act and Working with Local Authorities – A Guide for Parents
The Children Act and the Courts – A Guide for Children and Young People
The Children Act and You – A Guide for Young People
Getting Help From Social Services – A Guide for Children and Young People
The Children Act and the Courts – A Guide for Parents
The Children Act and Day Care – A Guide to the Law

The Children Act – A Guide to Help You With Day Care
Registration
All produced by the Department of Health and obtainable
from BAPS, Health Publications Unit, DSS Distribution
Centre, Heywood Stores, Manchester Road, Heywood,
Lancashire OL10 2PZ.

For further information on
basic or advanced training
supervision
training the trainers
youth leaders
supporting the hurt child
setting up a Christian centre
feasibility studies
consultancy

Contact: Roger Altman
Director of Barnabas Training Consortium
Salem Chapel
Salem Road
Johnstown
Carmarthen
Dyfed
SA31 3HJ
Tel: 01267 230428
Fax: 01267 221358